Mirror for You:
Collected Poems (1967-1999)

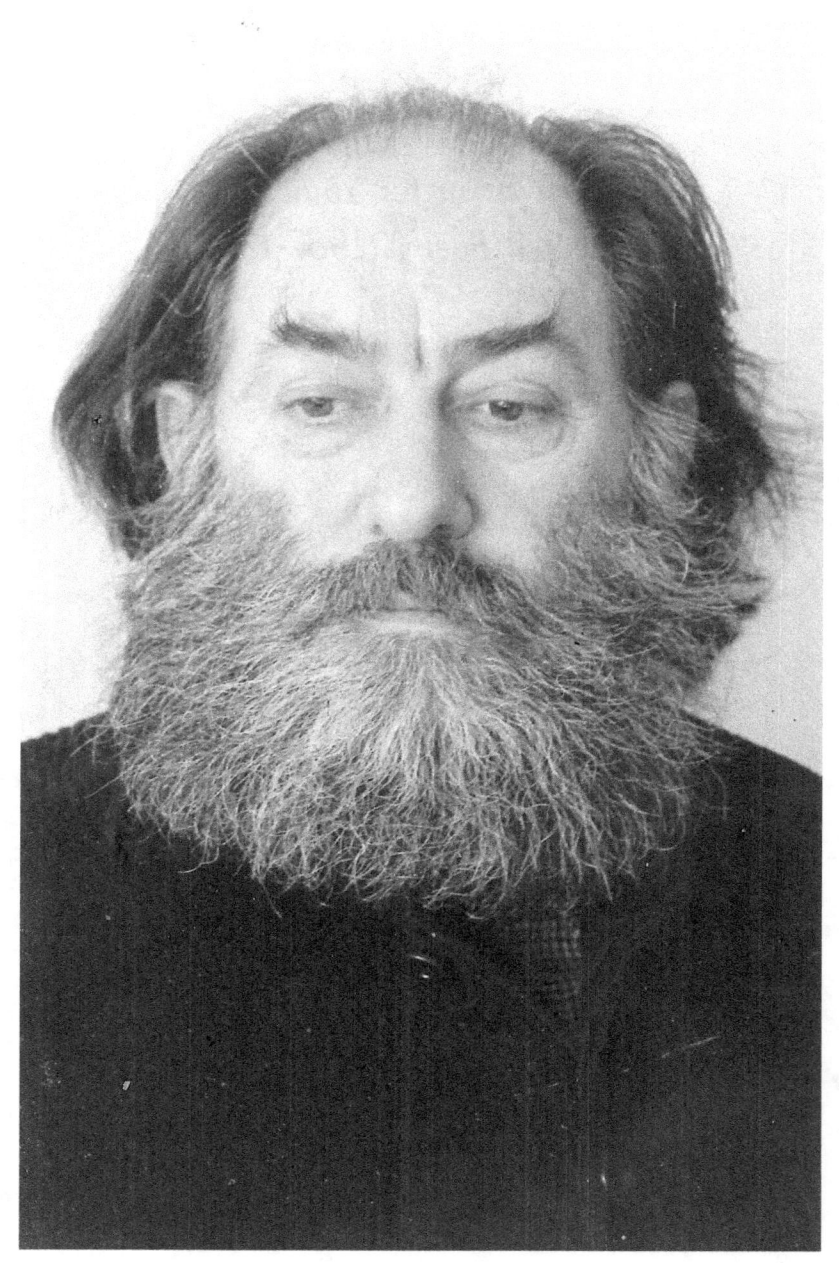

MIRROR FOR YOU
Collected Poems (1967-1999)

―――――

Elias Petropoulos

Translated from the Greek by John Taylor

Copyright © 2023 Mary Koukoules and the Estate of Elias Petropoulos. Nefeli Editions (Athens, Greece) is the publisher of the following books, from which these poems have been selected and translated:

Ποιήματα [Poems], 1980 / 1993
Topor: Τέσσερεις εποχές [Topor: Four Seasons], 1991
Ποτέ και τίποτα [Never and Nothing] and *Μετά* [After], 1993
Τέσσερεις ζωγράφοι [Four Painters], 1999, for the poems about Dimitris Souliotis's art

Copyright © 2023 John Taylor for the introduction, notes, and English translation

Cover illustration by Elias Petropoulos, photograph courtesy of Thanasis Moutsopoulos.
This collage, adapted for the front cover, is also included in Petropoulos's *Κυρίως αυτό* [Mainly That: Selected Collages], Nefeli Editions, 1994

The translator and the publisher would like to express their gratitude to Mary Koukoules for her help and encouragement during their work on this project

Page iv — photo of Elias Petropoulos by Vassilis Liappas, c. 1980

All rights reserved

ISBN: 978-0-646-87533-0

Published by Cycladic Press, Sydney, Australia

All Rights Reserved. No part of this book may be reproduced or transmitted in any form or by any means, electronic or mechanical, including photocopy, recording, or any information storage and retrieval system, without prior permission in writing from the publisher. All inquires should be addressed to Michael Alexandratos, Cycladic Press: cycladic.press@gmail.com

CONTENTS

"Mirrors of Melancholy: The Poems of Elias Petropoulos" An Introduction by John Taylor	ix
Funeral Oration	1
Body	23
Suicide	31
Five Erotic Poems	45
Tsoclis's Tree	53
Mirror for You	61
In Berlin: Notebook 1983-1984	67
Letter to A. Kanavakis	93
Inaccessible Tsoclis	99
An Encomium to Cicciolina	111
Four Seasons: Roland Topor	117
Never and Nothing	125
After	169
Ten Poems for Dimitris Souliotis	217
Notes	231

Mirrors of Melancholy
The Poems of Elias Petropoulos

This book offers the translation of nearly all the poetry and poetic prose written by the Greek poet and urban folklorist Elias Petropoulos (1928-2003). Included here are his initially complete *Poems* (1980 / 1993), his *Four Seasons* (1991) evoking the French artist Roland Topor, his double collection *Never and Nothing* and *After* (1993), and his ten poems (1999) inspired by the paintings of the Greek artist Dimitris Souliotis. Three poetic sequences in this book previously appeared in my translations during the 1980s, in deluxe limited bibliophilic editions illustrated by other artist-friends (Alekos Fassianos, Costas Tsoclis, and Michael Bastow). Long ago, *Body* and *Inaccessible Tsoclis* were published in English versions made by other hands; but, similarly, in an album and a catalogue that have become hard to find. It can therefore be said that *Mirror for You: Collected Poems (1967-1999)* represents the first time that Petropoulos's poetry has been made widely available in English.

The title of my book-length memoir of working with Petropoulos as his translator is *Harsh out of Tenderness* (2020). I borrowed the phrase from the opening autobiographical poem of *Never and Nothing*. As I was perusing all his poems for this project and translating most of them for the first time, the aptness of this self-description kept striking me again. Like the American poet Charles Bukowski (to whom he can be compared in some respects), Petropoulos had a sulfuric reputation throughout his career. His status as the troublemaker of Greek letters was quickly established, if not beforehand, by his three imprisonments during the Junta (1967-1974) on "pornography" charges: first, for anthologizing the genuine uncensored lyrics of Greek *rebetic* songs (1968); secondly, for one line in his long poem *Body* (1969); and, thirdly, for *Kaliarda* (1971), his dictionary of Greek homosexual slang. In such cases and several later ones, Petropoulos showed himself to be extremely brave in his personal combat against political repression and the inhibiting constraints of self-righteous morality. He himself sums up his stance in *Never and Nothing*:

> Anything that is against the Church
> rejoices me.
> Anything that damages the Established Order
> appeases me.
> Anything that opposes Morality
> is good for my health.

In light of such declarations, it is unsurprising that, as he was living in Paris (beginning in 1975) and as his controversial books were being both widely reviewed and sometimes savagely impugned in Greece, his personality was simultaneously assumed to be abrupt, aggressive, and aggravating, seemingly monomaniacal. Even technical aspects of his writing style could irritate, such as his mischievously inserted grammatical solecisms and predilection for capital letters (especially in his later poems), his abrupt interruptions of an unfinished line with a period (which, for syntactic clarity in English, I have sometimes replaced with an em-dash in my translations), or, as if he were stuttering, searching for words or just being refractory for fun, his intentional repetitions of simple words and conjunctions (like "and") at the end of one line and the beginning of the next line. If I may make an understatement, it's true that he could be hard to get along with—at least for some of his professional interlocutors. However, those of us who were close to him, and worked closely with him, perceived other qualities in his makeup, including much generosity and even a certain shyness.

In his poetry, he often exposes this sensitive side. It unfolds into much deeper layers than most people suspect. Petropoulos himself orients us in this direction when he remarks in *After*: "I know. / You see me as a thistle. / Open me more deeply, and you'll find me." For this reason alone, this volume will surely provoke unsettling and conflicting reactions in readers, who in the English-speaking world will be discovering the poet for the first time and pondering his inner complexity, let alone turmoil. Petropoulos's proverbial harshness surges forth in many pieces. This is especially realized in his "anti-poems," "poor poems," and "ugly poems," for which his "notebook" *In Berlin* (1987) purports to be a "manifesto." "I don't believe at all in Inspiration," he announces, "I consider Poetry to be mere Gymnastic Exercise." Yet not only in *In Berlin* but in all his poetry books he candidly puts forth his "melancholy" (a recurrent word), his fears (also omnipresent), his amorous yearnings and losses, and his lifelong grappling with death as well as with specific deaths: the probable, yet unelucidated, murder of his father during the Second World War; the deaths of friends as eye-witnessed during the Greek Civil War (in which he fought as a guerrilla on the Leftist side); and his own inevitable death, sometimes already envisioned in early poems as suicide. In brief, he contemplates *corpses, corpses, corpses* (1990)—as the title of one of his books puts it. One of my first translations of Petropoulos's writing was in fact made for his album of drawings *The Graves of Greece* (1979), a topic that obsessed him until his last days, when he died after a long struggle with prostate cancer. Significantly, *The Cemeteries of Greece*, a book which he claimed would be his masterpiece and on which he had probably begun to work well before the late-1970s, when he first spoke to me about the project, was left unfinished on his desk at his death. The book was published posthumously in 2005, with illustrations by Costas Tsoclis. "In my Fatherland, wherever you dig," he writes in one of his poems about Souliotis's art, "you'll find the bones of the slain." And in *Suicide* (1973): "My fatherland: wildflowers cover the murdered. / My fatherland, a hunting bag full of severed heads."

Alongside this death theme, eros pervades these poems and poetic prose texts. Eros defiantly stands up to Thanatos, while remaining (melancholily, once again) aware of the inexorable outcome of the combat. Usually, the eros depicted is joyfully genital, but then Petropoulos turns (in *Funeral Oration*, for example) to amorous emotions that surprise one with lines such as "Close me up in your heart and may only the two of us know" or "Do you still remember me, my departed love?" Most (but not all) of the time, Petropoulos praises Women—with a capital "W." He even pens an "encomium" to the porn star and erstwhile Italian parliamentary deputy Cicciolina (Ilona Staller). He recalls and imagines naked female bodies graphically yet also sometimes romantically. "Ah, what would be left to us if we lacked romance?" he states (in one of the poems devoted to Souliotis's paintings), albeit not without irony. More typically, however, he tends to view romantic and sexual longing matter-of-factly, as in his *Letter* to the artist Anakreon Kanavakis: "Contemporary Pornography is but the Romanticism of our Times." As this straightforward statement shows, Petropoulos's poetry can also be sternly, stubbornly prosaic. Aphoristic comments appear in many pieces, not only in those devoted to his artist-friends. Time and again he returns to his fundamental materialism, which is his essential philosophical orientation. In *After* he notably asserts: "All that exists is this Body you adore." Needless to say, it is unlikely that Petropoulos imagined any threshold or horizon beyond which might lie some form of transcendence. For him, what emerges from the hard facts of the body and the world of human beings is melancholy—and one will notice, in these poems, the importance given to feeling, not only to sensation. Moreover, his later poetry sometimes shows melancholy evolving into disgust, a more dire and debilitating state of emotion against which he struggled hard by laboring very long hours over his books-in-progress. "Men are faithful only to their work," he points out in *Body*.

Apropos of his vantage point on femaleness and feminism (which he satirizes here once or twice, as he does elsewhere, with a predilection for poking fun at the French novelist Marguerite Duras), it can be added that the author of *The Brothel*

(1980), *A History of the Condom* (1996), and *The Shit-Cutter, or The G-String* (2002)—to mention three more titles from among the seventy-odd books that he published—had an unfailing knack, not only for taking on taboo subjects a decade or two before it became fashionable among academics to write about them, but also for expressing himself with a forthrightness that ran up hard and abrasively against sensibilities increasingly—already by the end of the last century—molded by political correctness. Petropoulos was naturally, adamantly, roguishly, sometimes unjustly (it must be said), but also sometimes pertinently, "incorrect."

It goes without saying that some readers will deem these poems to be "phallocratic." The "phallo-" half of the equation is consistently present; the "cratic" variable, with its emphasis, via the Greek *kratos*, on "strength, might, and authority," is equally active, but more nuanced and faceted than it might seem upon a first reading. It indeed functions as a variable. How should these lines from *After* be read?

> . . . I've always been a slave,
> —I mean, the slave of Women.
> And I don't consider it humiliating
> to be dominated by a Woman.
> A true man knows how to let things be.
> Moreover, let me inform you that I'm no masochist.

And if Petropoulos likewise appears "gynophilic" in the ancient Greek sense of one who, like Zeus in Theocritus' *Idyll 8*, "lusts after women," and if he admits (in *Five Erotic Poems*) to being a "drug addict of pleasure," he also has a penchant for generalizations made half in jest, half in earnest. In *Body*, for instance, he notes that "a naked female body sparks a discussion about personality." Other lines or sentences illustrate less the poet's hedonism than his skepticism about valid, stable definitions. "Long live contradictory definitions," he exclaims in *Suicide*. His *Encomium to Cicciolina* includes this unsettling syllogism in which—as one of his other stylistic traits would have it—conventional transitions are conspicuously missing: "Specialists vainly seek to define the difference between Eroticism and Pornography. Definitions have a great attraction for academics. The word *vagina* begins with a V (like *victory*)." But consider this line in *Suicide*: "To syllogisms and arguments, I prefer screams." Or this neo-Cartesian maxim from *Funeral Oration*: "I contradict myself, therefore I live." Ultimately, Petropoulos applies his trenchant skepticism about definitions to the definitions and self-definitions that he himself formulates. This is what he avows in *After*: "I see the Truth in others; / I am cross-eyed in front of my own Truth."

All told, we should probably take him at his word when he confesses in *Never and Nothing* that he has "never been unhappy. / I get along well with my / innate melancholy." Like many other lines or sentences in this book, this self-description can of course be read ironically, or unironically, or from both angles at once. In his first book, *Nikos Gabriel Pentzikis* (1958), didn't he offer this tribute to his mentor? "Pentzikis showed me how to use my eyes. Slowly but surely I learned how to see things askew, diagonally, illogically, axonometrically, unorthodoxly." In *Funeral Oration*, he admitted: "I would never have been able to think without melancholy nearby." Petropoulos wrote until the very last moment, when physical incapacity forced him to set down his felt-tipped pen, push his manual typewriter off to the side of his desk, and enter the Clinique Geoffroy Saint-Hilaire, a few streets down the hill from the rue Mouffetard apartment. His last controversial act, as outlined in his "testament"—one of the poems from *Never and Nothing*—was to have his ashes thrown into a sewer after his cremation at the Père Lachaise Cemetery. This took place and I was present. A characteristically uncomfortable self-portrait emerges from these disturbing pages. Such was the man—and such is the poet and his potent poetry. In addition, whether we like it or not, this self-portrait holds out a mirror to us—that "Truth in others" he pinpointed in *After*. Therefore, in this English-language volume, the at once introverted and extraverted overarching title of *Mirror for You*, which Petropoulos himself chose for his most playfully provocative book. It sums up one of his deepest literary intentions and most lasting accomplishments.

John Taylor
Saint-Barthélemy d'Anjou
26 June 2022

............Funeral Oration............

for the old unknown rebetic songs
but at the same time an Elegy
in memory of the beauty of an
eminently beloved Woman

Rebetic songs are called the chants of the wounded,
of the simple, naïve, and sensitive souls of Greece.
Rebetic songs tell remarkably well
      of scorned unrequited love
            and the great martyrdom of willingly buried eros.
Rebetic songs were once our consolation.
They were the pure white embraces of the unrecognized.
I had the honor of holding General Makriyannis's
    now-mute bouzouki.
Rebetic songs were not sung by women
    (who usually understand only later how much they were loved),
        nor by hard hearts.

I care not only for truth
        but also for the beauty of truth.
Don't send me turtle doves
        —I can guess the words of love you'll say.
Eros takes place accidently.
Back then I held your body like a violin,
        but now that we're far away from each other,
                the fire in my heart for you keeps burning.
You'll sadly search for me in the deserted streets
        and will ask about me everywhere
                and in the enveloping melancholy of rebetic songs
                      you'll seek consolation in vain.
This year it rained on Easter
        and treachery embittered my heart.

I know: my place is in the cemetery.
We were still children when they shriveled us up
      and we lived like old people.
I'm not myself.
I keep silent, but I refuse to die
      because your teary eyes keep blinking at me.
Wretched gazes, children of my silence.
Tonight death drives everything out of my soul.
I rejoice in my insanity now.

The true weight of a man is equal to his loves,
        the pity and disgust he felt in life.
I experienced two great injustices:
        poverty and erotic contempt.
Rebetic songs have been promoted to a mausoleum of emotions.
To bear the bitterness of this world is necessary,
        and perhaps justified.
Passion I gave and passion I did not receive,
        and whatever I took hold of became ash.
I was taught a lot by rebetic songs.
My father suckled me on them.
I built my book about rebetic songs
        (as if I were building a swallow's nest)
                for the sake of my lifelong friend Vassilis Tsitsanis.
Rebetic songs taught me patience.

I'm burying myself today.
I'm snuffed out (ah, snuffed out) when you use my feelings
      like coins.
If it's a matter of someone maintaining his sensitivity
      he'll be the loser.
Rebetic songs prosper as memories.
We lived through the most nightmarish nights of the century.
Reminders are lurking.
I felt everything only as passion.
Let me be a madman,
      since logic is the vestibule of madness.
I was an Ideal Faun.
I will tear you down with tears, gloomy beloved woman.

Rebetic songs are songs of the heart.
And only one who approaches them with innocent feeling is moved
      by them, delights in them.
Because the heart is measured by the heart.

The cycle of rebetic songs has come to a close.
Those songs now belong to the past.
I'm mourning mortally at their memorial service,
    since Mikis Theodorakis wavers tonight
        between euphemism and subsistence.

Creation suddenly darkens
and suicide turns out to be every wise man's dream.
Goddess-bearing eros is life's only persuasion.
I stood in front of heart-shaped amulets in the Byzantine Museum
    of Athens.
On the hairy arms of rebetes
    you often see a many-leafed heart
        with the beloved woman's name in the middle.

For centuries Modern Greeks were pregnant with rebetic songs.
In the act of love, time was imposed on men
After we were born, death remained.
I drank the thousand bitter no's, before I gulped down rebetic songs.
Joys, like pleasures, lead to genuine sorrow.
Like gestures of vehement lamentation, they resemble the fluttering wings
    of those dancing the *zeybekiko*.
Yiannis Tsarouchis knows that the *zeybekiko* is called
    the Dance of all Dances.
Perhaps only someone in love
could compose the funeral oration for the rebetic songs,
        which continue to seem
        a remote magical flower garden,
        definitively lost and inaccessible.
The minds of men
    (as potent as love, omnipotent as death)
    are projected towards the past.
Sorrow is the echo of erotic folksongs.
May Greek children soon be taught in schools
    the incomparable melancholy of rebetic songs.

From what remains, I'll make a career out of being a traitor.
Deeply for me, deeply for you, we hurt our hearts.
My sighs kept me awake all night long.
I am a friend of the dead.
The next passion saves me from the previous one,
      but each passion
             settles in my palimpsest soul like blackness,
                    and then suicide plays the role of redemption.
Genius is the only acceptable form of insanity,
      or the commiserate burden of other people's misfortunes.
Great loves, all of them, are like erotic laments.
Love lacks victory.
It begins and ends with the defeat of the man.
Like Achilles, you were proud and hard-hearted
      —but the time is ripe, wherever you are
           my sweet darling.

Like a lost dog, a stray dog,
      I slink through these dark days with an empty heart
           and every twilight I fall, fall, into an abyss I fall.
Of course, women lack imagination and passion,
      but I loved and was loved,
      and I can show you, when I am asked, the meaning of eros.
Like a deserter among the myriads in the desert of Athens,
      where I am terrified and everything pushes me towards suicide.
Pessimism is a proof of humanity.
I am my enemy.
At the age I have reached, I clearly sense
      that I am a failure.
I would never have been able to think without melancholy nearby.
I often steal souls,
      but you're not near me, nor in a stranger's hands.
I grew old with a teenager's erotic heart.
It's outrageous to live with love
           and perilous to possess so thoroughly
                the secrets of your soul.
It's impossible to bury the memories
           and this will determine my death.
I saw my grave bed.
How many days, how many years, would you stand a life without hopes?

You're late in coming; my soul freezes.
In the evenings I sit all alone, deeply alone, in the little room
                                        you know,
                          and I blame myself
                                  and keep thinking
            about the relentless wear and tear of feelings
My mind wanders towards despair.
Once, many friends of mine were killed in my midst
        and ever since, I live like a terrorized bird.
I wait for you day and night, and expect with every dawn
        that you'll return.
My heart gets carried away
                            (you, my sweetheart, still rule it)
            into reminiscing about your exquisite shapeliness,
                    which I cannot and do not want to forget,
                    and which, once lost, threw me into black darkness.
The woman sitting across from me—I have her in my chest.

The shadows of murdered friends, and last night,
    like every night,
        they came slowly writhing in my sleep,
            and just as soon you were with them, half-hidden,
        speechless, shriveled-up.
Revering their memory, I wander around the Street of Repose.
When the beloved woman leaves, it is as if she has died.
In your eyes the signs of betrayal.
A woman's beauty a garment of pleasure.
Close me up in your heart and may only the two of us know.

Rebetic songs flourished in the days when we were counting graves.
Action wears down a man almost completely.
Rebetes hate moderates.
Wise is he who loves and hopes
      and very wise he who grieves.
The lover ends up half human.
Pity should be considered the convalescence of love.
Inhabitants of the earth: learn about love.
The disappointed always save the universe.
A special kind of bravura is required for one to be immoral.
My logic resides in my heart.
Love nourishes (alas) ideals.
Things of the past are glorified.
Cynicism seems to be the breastplate of the sensitive,
      protecting them from the demon of introspection.
Pity comes along with the years.
Thought is misfortune.
I sin out of pity.

I'm frightened when I think.
You were so beautiful that I respected you.
Even the negator who refuses to pass away is reactionary.
I contradict myself, therefore I live.
Suicide is the reciprocated expression of the social punishment
    of psychic exorcism.
The only personal act in suicide
    is the voluntary execution of a social decision.
In a man's love, the warm blessed feeling probably matters more
    than the beloved woman's name.
My head, now, on a coffin headrest,
    and not, now, resting on your knees.
I traced the sign of the cross on your forehead.
Solitude caress of death.

Her eyes foretold the condemnation.
The separation cost me nothing; nothing but
    the enthronement of melancholy.
There are probably no disinterested women in love.
A woman aspires to be the undertaker of her beloved.
Deaths and deaths will pass, but you will last within me.
You who are absent and yet whom I feel looking at me with a thousand
    eyes.
You who were the one with the bitter tears
    and sweet kisses.
You, the brilliant one, who compelled me to love flowers
    more than human beings.
You, the wolf-eater and the angel of earthly meadows.

They did everything to shrivel up the living heart
    of the rebetes.
Great souls contradict themselves.
The strongest memory is the heart's memory.
Lyricism was the only luxury that rebetic singers were allowed.
Like refreshing foliage, tenderness surrounds former feelings.
Once again, on the edge of the cliff,
    I change my soul and my mind blossoms.
A Calvin of pure eros, I hope how and—
    and the most ruthless beloved woman
        cannot kill the poetry
            that hides inside a silent man.

Basically, rebetic songs are folksongs of love and,
        especially, of erotic abandonment.
At least half of the rebetic songs have eros for a theme,
        and most of them mourn amorous separation
              —the bitterest orphanhood.
The rebetis knows that love is a transferable feeling
              and that the masters' pity is love.
The rebetes felt passion so much
        that they lost the right to represent themselves.
In demotic folksongs, the lover amazes with his virility,
        while the lover of rebetic songs begs,
            implores, attracts through pity.
Rebetic songs transformed triumphant love into a litany
        in which embraces are psychic
            and memories dominate.

It happens that I clearly understand the erotic archpriest,
                        that if you don't build a life of mistakes and sins
                              you will not be subject to death,
             that it's definitely better to be killed than to kill yourself,
                  since the vast invincible majority of nasty people
                            never felt greed nor tender fear,
                and, that the heart is the house of the soul.
Lust is a true disease.
Your naked body (jubilation of my eyesight)
      leads to autumn, to autumn.

Essentially, rebetic songs are love letters.
A human being is dual.
I recall you only as a beautiful girl
                              (oh, the majesty of tall women)
                              coming with an armful of flowers,
                    and then I kissed you and you kissed
                    me back,
                              you my faith and my hope.
I loved a cypress tree, the hitherto unknown woman who is not forgotten.
The Feast of the Dead, the day of separation.
You said everywhere that you hated me, but when we met again,
                    for the last time,
          you wept and tenderly spread
          your precious ivory hand over my sweaty forehead.
Now you're flying nearby—as far away from me as ever.
Do you still remember me, my departed love?

Lovers use pure-gold words,
      words that burn,
           even if the love is felt and they cannot prove it.
Lovers express themselves with hyperboles,
      because they live in hyperbole.
Even if a man has a mountain of a heart,
      he is unable to love many times in his life.
Eros is a bittersweet nightmare, a shroud for the living,
      a murderer, a tyrannizer,
           a pallbearer of birds, a liberator.
Such loves are sung by my brothers, the last rebetes.

....Body..

That's the way it is: a naked woman is a sad sight.
Unfortunately, I'm still sane.
Art has its own morals.
Beauty, the legality of nature.
In front of a naked female body, little children are amazed
                                  and true tender men are terrified.
A naked female body sparks a discussion about personality.
Body of the greatest sweetness, devastating envelope.
Body of day and midnight; body of consolation.
It's not reasonable that everyone sees beautiful women naked;
give not that which is holy unto the dogs, neither cast ye your pearls before swine.
Deep inside me a battle wages.
Vision means ideal possession.
Life is mute isn't it. I demand dreams.
My sorrow constitutes my happiness.
Body, it's you who are the soul.
       O memorable vulva.
       O double-lipped slit with its silvery moisture.

Love cannot be forgotten through hate.
Hate fatally comes as an award for eros.
Anything that pleases me is moral.
Erotic pleasure limits conflict with oneself.
A woman on a sofa looks like a wild beast lying down,
                                        and reverie feeds it.
Every corpse is the negation of a body.
Look me in the eyes, Lady of mine, and listen to this epitaph
you asked me for:
                        HERE LIES
                  THAT BEAUTIFUL ONE
                    GONE FOREVER
          WITHOUT TAKING MY PAIN WITH HER
Where eros ends begins condescendence ends where—
Today an erotic act is considered to be an exercise.
Every day that fades away, every dawn that comes,
                                      intensifies my disrespect.
Ugly bodies are characteristic.
May female beauty be prohibited at last.
Eros gets rid of sadness through pleasure.
The act of coitus is the summit of egotism the—
I know nothing more melancholy than a completely naked female body.
    O vulva, odeon of orphans, Horn of Amalthea,
    my sheath, Scylla and Charybdis.

It's not your body but my feelings that I dissect.
Each body is a codicil.
Your crown your hate.
Your body tells only death stories.
Pleasure, the echo of Never.
As to you, you grow silent; but I discover you.
Our true moments are moments of solitude.
Like flowers, every female body has its odor.
Death is the only worthy act of the body.
I don't know where I belong where—
A man with an impious heart doesn't delight in the beauty
                        of a female body, its grace.
Pleasure, the smile of the perfect act.
Stretched out naked with her necklace of tears on her breasts,
                  she thinks that beauty is the alms given by nature.
Be lenient with the body's impulses.
I am not responsible for the evil that I commit.
I hardly believe in the intellectuality of women.

In love we are all autodidacts.
Eros is not a target.
Men are faithful only to their work.
Men consider eros to be an allegorical pause.
Forgetfulness, that immoral mechanism, forgetfulness.
The beautiful dead woman is probably unable to boast about herself.
I forget even my fatherland in front of a young naked female body.
The presence of a woman imposes meditation.
Indeed, it's only a myth: the so-called plenitude provided by eros.
Jealousy is the recompense that a lover gives to his beloved.
In our age, literature has worn down even the sexual act.
Eros did not ask us whether we consented.
Anatolians, through a millennial tradition,
    had the most inalterable system of ownership for the female body.
The body of a woman is an optical phenomenon
    that impetuously tends to become a tactile fact.
Copulation is combat. Only in darkness am I unafraid.
Death rattle, copulation.
    O sacred repugnant vulva.
    O snake-mother and snake-hole and snake-nest.
    O anti-beauty vulva, propylaea of boredom.
    O sweet punishment.

In front of a naked woman, men are much shier than one thinks.
Embrace me and drown me; obscenity is my pride.
For the whims of my beloved, I become the Lernaean Hydra.
The drama of the human soul comes from
      the obligatory pardon that provides everyone with his
      own immorality.
Hatred eros blackness.
The ideal erotic act ends in tears.
I kiss your eyes, because you also sense that eros
              consists of an inacceptable fault of nature.

Two lovers two accomplices two.
Whoever gives himself over to fate lives in truth.
But you can even save up your sentiments.
Now I love you and now I sense that I am sprouting leaves.
I adorn your moist armpits with jasmine.
                (Is a lover a bearer of conscience?)
The veneration of female beauty has something animalistic about it.
Beauty, a youthful ambition.
    O vulva, the devil's funnel.
    O vulva, glorious water sink.
    O vulva, Mecca of my thoughts.
    O Macedonian sky.

From love derives melancholy,
                and yet melancholy crushes love.
Pleasure, remote vengeance of Time.
Misanthropes call the friends of mankind misanthropes.
The grammar of kisses is as indispensable
                            as the grammar of words.
A bad victory, the copulation of bodies.
The future will tell if eros means the exasperation
                            of mores and feelings.
Of all this—and more that frightens me and that I cannot write down—
I think when I see naked women.

....**Suicide**..

To Mary

I happen to be an atheist, but I consider those who kill themselves
to be children of God.
Christian liturgy doesn't provide a funeral oration for suicides.
He who kills himself is a mortal who insinuates his way into
divine works
                          —I'm speaking ironically here.
Every state without good laws should decree the arrest
                of all those who refuse to kill themselves.
I don't care about the morality of the tactic.
The good strategist is not interested in the enemy target.
My strategy is unavowable.
Therefore, I kill myself out of strategy.
He who wants to kill himself employs persuasion
           against himself in the way that a lover persuades himself.
The idea of killing himself enthuses him and terrorizes him.
Silent foliage conceals my ideas and illogicality
              envelops my reflections—this is what they say.
It is in extreme seriousness and clarity that the suicide
                          lives his last hours.
All the dreams of man are fulfilled
          in the coffin. I spit truths and—
He who kills himself is the lord of sadness.

A Jesus for every day because.
The ambitious human being is an egoist; glory, the highest self-interest.
The suicide is negatively egoistic,
                            offers everything for the minimum.
In the soul of every worthy man crouches counter-opposition.
Killing myself (I think) means: I exert absolute power against myself.
The suicide no longer remained a partisan of himself.
Whoever succumbs to temptations fears suicide.
Obviously, I'm not writing an apology for suicide.
My suicide seduces me. No one borrows death.
Shatter forms before they form a shell.
Big coffin: great sadness;
                    a child's small coffin: the greatest sadness.
I was born in Greece—this is the only favor I have received from the goddess Fortuna.
The suicide, perpetual to-and-fro.
However, even the most beautiful woman cannot chase away
the dark thoughts
            of a melancholy man.

A little before the desired death, the suicide changes his smile.
I will rot away in the grave; and even then I won't understand.
NOTHING IN EXCESS. I'm tired of your scholastic adages.
When the perfect circle creates two centers, suicide comes closer.
You've killed me with sharp cutting words.
KNOW THYSELF. How those shitty sayings bore me.
Socrates' suicide, putting his wisdom into practice.
I'm not interested in definitions based on proof.
A proof is a schema and a definition is an oracle.
For me: everything that bears my signature is equivalent to a proof:
    for you.
Sometimes the main thing in a suicide is how it is done.
There are even suicide stylists.
Suicide appears to be the total, definitive passion
    since its climax coincides with the death of the one who
    is passionate.
By killing myself, I actually remain myself.
(I laughed, laughed a lot, until my eyes filled with tears, until I started weeping).

Suicide is a prologue and possesses no imagination no—
Imagination is more frightful than reality.
Knowledge turns towards and against us.
I continue to live because I continue to pretend.
Only people lacking finesse kill themselves
              for material or purely exterior reasons.
                          —this is how your Mr. Dostoyevsky spoke.
He who kills himself in an undisciplined way often offends us.

Save me from myself.
Let's henceforth think, not with words, but with screams.
Some people who take their life by their own hand don't take it by their own hand
                        —essentially, Hamlet killed himself.
My sensibility is equivalent to my disrespect.
I gave up on vanquishing; now I'll vanquish you.
He who kills himself is the Eternal Archpriest.
The Prime Magister and the Pontifex Maximus
                        The Last Centaur and the Centurion
                                The Merciful One
                    The Speared One and the Javelined One
                                    The October
                                   The Athenian
                        The Perpetually Afflicted One.

Let your kisses fly at me.

Birth; suicide: at the four cardinal points suicide.
Deadman, you take from me what you don't give me.
The suicidal man will sleep in our hearts.
I forgive even crimes. But I have friends who never forgive—
 those poor fellows—not even spelling mistakes. Yet fate decrees.
I remember my dead friends and my soul weeps.
One night under a full moon I'll frightfully go into the forest, a night
with the moon.
Suicide is the noblest of vengeances.
Give me flowers now; I don't want them on my grave.
I despaired, you go and kill yourself.
Every day we weep less and less, and this withers humanity.
If I wish, I can speak clearly, but when I'm afraid I change into
the Pythia.
The suicidal person possesses the power to revoke
 (Eternal Archpriest, you are pure)
and he deposes his soul
 (you crafty Prime Magister).
The effect suffices for me: it comes down. I head not towards conclusions.
The heart is more precious than the mind and the soul is centered
in the heart.
I kill myself means I refuse to remember.
 (My fatherland: wildflowers cover the murdered.
 My fatherland, a hunting bag full of severed heads.
 My fatherland—my horror!)

Today, battles are impersonal and
                                      suicide is the price of failure.
If he who kills himself by his own hand looks like a hero,
                                      few of those heroes were ever glorified.
A friend kills himself;
                  a good, select, sensitive human being has disappeared.
Not a second have I lived in peace.
Shame on he who has never thought, not even once in his life,
                                                  of killing himself.
He who kills himself is a passive anarchist.

In every moment, another definition. Long live contradictory definitions.
For centuries now, Greeks have lost the dual form.
But for the suicidal man, the plural has also vanished.
The application of casuistry to factual suicide
leads to hours of solitude leads to hours of remorse leads—
He who takes his life by his own hand didn't play as a child. I act to avoid thinking.
Sophistic suicide against one's body and the absolute beyond
of introspection.
Hopes do not visit he who kills himself hopes—
                  hopes hopes cradle of the soul hopes—
I actually don't know a more justified ambition than suicide
(through which one can deify oneself).
Every man has the age of his penis.
Every man hides a queer inside him.
(Coffins of killed protestors lined up on the ground.
      Someone was speaking, making a speech.
      I was seven years old—back then).
Wrong is he who thinks that a candidate for suicide is unhappy.
He who kills himself has vainly sought a soothsayer.
He who kills himself is the only one who has convinced his other self.
He who kills himself doesn't seem as ridiculous as Epicureans think.
He who kills himself by his own hand is an underground beast.
He who kills himself, death enclosed.
First a refusal, and then a new refusal.
(O long inner discussion with the frightful ending).

The candidate for suicide is a human being and the human being is dead
    and the dead man is no longer a human being and he who has
    killed himself
                                  doesn't exist as a non-human being.
I've lived all my life (alas) by chance.
A work of art is a means of defense.
Classify suicide among pleasures; it is the great absolution.
Death has its odor and several times I have smelled it.
No one chooses his cross.
The mediocre persuade the mediocre.
I am my death. I live with memories, thus, defensively.
ΝΙΨΟΝΑΝΟΜΗΜΑΤΑΜΗΜΟΝΑΝΟΨΙΝ
Wash the sins, not only the face. Suicide exalts melancholy
and stimulates the feeble. Νίϕον μόνον όϕιν ανομημάτων.
Wash only the face of sins.
Suicide as an arbitrary act is not to be generalized.
Those who take themselves by their own hand usually act as autodidacts
        (don't speak to me about a predisposition)
    and this polite act provokes no hatred.
Friendly fellows are also those who use a scorpion to kill themselves.
He who takes his life by his own hand opens a royal road, strolls down it.

A suicide is actually a moral fact.
Practically speaking, the fact can resonate all the way down to
the descendants.
Miserable survivors, don't linger over the suicide technique
                 and its apparent categories of motives;
                         suicide is a means and a result, never a goal.
I forget those who mistreat me.
Experience arms the dying and experience binds.
He who kills himself is an auto-dynamic, auto-mechanical automaton.
Every one of my sighs is a sentence but.
Some think that the lack of money
                 is even the crux of a suicide because of love.
However, we don't exactly know why human beings kill themselves and—
The pensive man who takes his life by his own hand
                   he who remains silent despite his glaring act
he who terminates the contradiction and he who returns the promise
                     the solitary shepherd the immaculate one
       and he should not be mourned by those close to him
                                 the lovers.

To syllogisms and arguments, I prefer screams.
I kill myself because pains and pleasures have run dry.
Executioner of himself, he who takes his life by his own hand
lacks humor.
Suicide (according to your comfortable viewpoint)
          is a catastrophic synthesis of conflictual psychic tendencies;
                    and death to the infinite power.
The evil of suicide weighs down on the survivors,
whereas the good is buried with the suicide.
I will be perpetually in love because I don't believe in my lucky star.
Suicide is not contemptible
but the face of evil.

        Let the curtain fall, my sweet suicidal person
                —shoot your pistol.

..................................Five Erotic Poems..................................

panting and panting I move in and out
woman you're smiling at me your legs gaping
whisperings in the ear
I know you through these spasms of yours
you're staring waiting staring into my eyes
you're staring waiting
I live with a rope around my neck
floweret flower-petal palm I fondle
bridal chamber and mooring rope
rope pistil, my angel, with your headful of hair
dead dog you're still secretly biting me
and ripping my heart
and I hate you and crave you
and I crave you and push you away
and panting and panting I slip inside sweetly forgetting

flee when you see an ugly woman flee
you I lie down with you me
and alongside is that Italian
pre-classical iridescence of music
and alongside is the pagan from Skiathos
the famous poor short-story writer
and all those alongside are lamenting
all those murdered friends
—I know those unforgettable faces—
I recall neither their names nor their nicknames
let dogs eat the ugly women
and the witches (who tyrannized me since)

You hide me under the bedsheets
when pleasure arrives from fabulously faraway
an earthquake of bodies is pleasure pleasure
dressed as you are in your skin
of smooth cool preoccupations you
the wind red curtains with softly waving stripes
and I play with words and place them like colors
mental parade saviors inestimable poets
Manto Aravantinou Priestess of Writings
The Other One who killed himself near the waves
Kostas Mavroudis the student poet
nor do I forget the bitter Nikos Karouzos
the same bitterness floats in Xexakis's soul
—patience, Manolis, patience dear friend
because the shabby bastards will shamelessly crush you

I was told at school that that
Art purifies the female body
and ancient statues were white pure white
and I mustn't be naughty
and the completely naked painted beauties
those pure virgin maidens of the Renaissance
(oh, teacher, why are you burying me alive?)
Art arouses no lowly appetites—insist the dimwits
mores morals morality my boy—they keep insisting
but I the misfit can glimpse an erotic position
even in the way a woman smokes

an erotic topic in Art arouses I vibrate
the theme of eroticism in a work of art
must must arouse (why not, for devil's sake?)
art imposes an erotic topic on me
Oh Solomos's icy women who are not women
and Sikeliotis's girls I crave you
my force can be measured in failures
an anarchist, you know, is repudiated even by his mother

what does I love mean what does it mean
body what does coitus mean it means what
throw out that hideous woman
throw out that angelic ox now
throw out that nereid of a buffalo and I'm disgusted
disgusted because I have survived my friends (they were brave)

I tag along behind very beautiful girls.
And I'm not ashamed of this don't regret it
PU PUD DEN DE ENDA DENDA
UD NDA DENDA UDENDA PUDENDA
I turn around and come back
and if I fail to return it's the end death
because I am a drug addict of pleasure

soft stomach white like milk
her hair hiding her pillow
and like this she is lying melting and fragrant
and I approach and am burning
—an indescribable sight, yes

Sikeliotis, you called and I came
to your studio—do you remember?—early one winter morning
while it was raining and drenched with melancholy
and I saw even my soul rejoicing
and all around everywhere I see hanging
meaningful monochromatic drawings
generously callipygian girls
fallen to the ground
I saw girls lying around
the swaying harem set down on paper
an ideal perfumed paradise—all your own
but let me see please let me
see how you capture
the shape of a female and her body how
you outline it how you possess it Sikeliotis how

my dear, I'm of course not shivering with emotion
like Andreas Embirikos
but with your voice I also touch the body
your glances my glances my perpetual sweet commotion
the superb smell of the roots of your hair
I want to caress every beautiful woman I see
unfortunately I don't shiver like Andreas Embirikos
his syllables are waves and waves and I'm jealous because
Embirikos is as erotic and I hate him

    (Yiorgos, my greetings to Mrs. Sikeliotis
    as well as to your daughters)

ugliness gives me a slap
medical terms make my heart freeze
bushy Pubis blackening into a Delta
Big Lips and silky Little Lips
moist Entrance moist Vagina
its Spongy Muscle that squeezes me down there
male and female Frenula
and Vaginal Membranes and Mucus
and other such horrors

I've never asked for advice and advice I am given
by uninvited advisors petit-bourgeois windbags
they say they say and keep prophesizing
that I'll be eaten by the gorgeous women
but it's my joy to be eaten by beauties
and, alas, you are the unfortunate ones
who don't eat your fill
and your life is founded on silence and sadness
as to me
        I love her on the sly and she is beautiful
and she is elegant and I kiss her secretly
not a bird spots us
not a flower overhears us
we kiss and the walls bend
weeping tears a salty taste at the gate
at the Gate of Consolation

(ah, pudenta trap pudenda tomb)

....Tsoclis's Tree..

He looks at me inquisitively and so I say: Let's go
      visit Tsoclis's atelier in the Marais.
He inquires: Is Tsoclis a Dorian or an Ionian?
I reply: Tsoclis is a Greek
      and a Greek is born weary.
When I use the Greek language,
I try to keep our cultural heritage from showing through, but
every Greek must vomit back up what he has inherited.
      —this Greek cultural heritage weighs heavy on one's stomach.
I can survive only by screaming: *Fuck the Parthenon!*
This is what I love about Jews,
Italians, and Armenians. The greatest Jewish revolutionaries
      would pop into a synagogue now and then.
Still incredulous, he inquires further: But does your Tsoclis
      paint abstract or figurative pictures?
Rather irritated, I reply: Not *my* Tsoclis,
      Tsoclis's Tsoclis. What Tsoclis is painting now
      will catch on in Greece ten years from now.
To be aware of the cultural heritage doesn't mean *I have to accept the cultural heritage.*
Across the room from my desk hangs a painting by Tsoclis.
                                        I bought it.
But it has belonged to me only since I have begun to understand it.
I want to talk about that Cultural Heritage.
You can't wipe it out with a conspiracy.
I fix my eyes on Tsoclis's large white painting
      with the Tree, the Tree, Tree.
The perspective gives an illusion of the Renaissance.
Tsoclis's board gives an illusion of a tree.
But the tree is not kept captive by the painting's border.

In a painting by Tsoclis, usually only one object is present,
                floating in a generally chromatic composition.
A real tree is the motive behind the painted tree.
                But a motive cannot be explained.
I approach the real tree in the real forest.
Tsoclis's tree has another code. Tsoclis refuses
                to bear the Past like a hamal who. . .
He interrupts me: But Tsoclis's painting is so simple.
                You're speaking as coherently as a Phythian.
I reply: You're right. So let's head over to Tsoclis's atelier
                to see his latest paintings
                and hear what he himself has to say. But
                let's go on foot. Art can be as potent
                as poison. Only the strongest, most sudden
                impressions can bring us close to it.

The sun is shining.
Sunny Paris is glorious Paris.
We walk down out of the Latin Quarter.
Street images.
A ravishing woman walks in front of us
      (what celestial swing!),
a police car siren, two Algerians
          speaking Arabic, we stroll around the back of Notre Dame
             (the cathedral's most beautiful side),
and on the *passerelle* children are roller-skating,
pont Louis-Philippe, rue des Écouffes,
I buy some sesame-seed cookies,
we stop outside of No. 20. Now we step into a cave.
Tsoclis's home looks like a train: one room, another room,
        a kitchen, the atelier.
Bonjour. Bonjour. Would you two like a cup of coffee?

And suddenly Tsoclis puts it to him: Why did you want
                                    to see my paintings?
Take a look at this one. I ended up being a journalist.
My objectivity is imaginary.
It's a leap I take inside the description of the object.
Taking the tree's hard shell in hand, I ossify Time.
I employ few words and a simple syntax.
Out of vengeance, I refuse to use a variety of colors. That is,
the whitish background weakens our censorship
                    of the painted object.
If you stick your nose up against an object
            you don't see it anymore. Ruskin proved that
            while speaking even about moving objects
            such as clouds.
I see a tree (-in-itself)
            as thick foliage and a wooden beam, because
I see a human being (-in-himself)
                as a divine creature and a future corpse.
Don't touch the painting!
I said that I was depicting the Tree-Idea, the Tree-Image.
Just look. Look.

Startled, the man inquires: Monsieur Tsoclis,
                                        do you like folk art?
The artist replies: I'm no monsieur. An able artist
remains an ideological bum.
Folk Art creeps along ever so slowly.
Was Socrates a man of the people?
In many ways, so-called Fine Art stands in opposition
                                        to Folk Art.
Picassos don't paint for a folk.
When I'm painting, I'm programming Utopia.
The terms *Folk* and *Folk Art*
            are political weapons.
The notion of a *Folk* is a ripped-up jacket.
Neither the notion of *Folk* nor that of *Folk Art*
            can be defined.
I'm not hanging onto the tail of Folk Art.
Severity is the gentility of our century.

..................................Mirror for You......................................

the first poem is serious

The eyes, the Mirror of the Soul.
I think it's a beautiful beginning for a poem,
                        with such an insipid line.
X wrote: *the loneliness of Paris is—*
                is the greatest loneliness in the world.
So true. But it's also true that
                Parisian ladies have devastating derrieres.
Today I'm sitting in the glass-enclosed terrace of the Atrium,
and whenever a hot number passes by, I turn,
twist around in my seat and watch her from behind,
for I'm a Greek and for a Greek what counts
                      is rump in a woman.
Ah, an anarchist can very well be a sodomite too.
At any rate, Christians set fine examples.
I don't believe in Universal History, as I don't believe
                don't believe in so-called Great Poetry.
The famed Homeric simile crystalizes an
                instant, an instantaneous image.
An epic, instants by the thousands. Homer, images by the tens of
thousands.
Schoolbooks didn't teach me a thing about the Belle Époque.
I scrutinize the events of 1900 in old
                        faded postcards.
              No mirrors are everlasting.

the second poem, with Alexander

The mirror punishes Narcissus.
The Moon Goddess is compared to a silvery mirror.
Sappho stammers: THE MOON HATH SET (etc.)
AND I SLEEP ALONE. (You deserve it, old tart).
But what stands in front of me isn't Sappho,
just this television set on the little table.
I'm lying on a Turkish divan with nine cushions,
hypnotically watching a ballerina on TV
and then two women playing tennis
and then a Russian lass figure skating.
The ballerina raises her leg above her head
and I'm hoping secretly that she'll split
her panty open so that her pussy will show
             (for even a ballerina has a pussy),
and then *The Dying Swan* is over,
and now I'm watching the tennis match
             (ogling, that is, at those round little tails),
and now, and now, still on the same show,
I'm gaping at the Soviet skater, as I said above.
Alexander asks me on the phone: She has
a beautiful body. Do you think she'd pose in the nude?
I reply: She already said she would,
but only if I'm present.
Alexander queries: Are you a peeping Tom too?
I explain: But you don't understand. I'm going to fuck her
             and while I'm fucking her you're going to paint.
       Your Venetian mirror already clouds over.

the third poem has a hard-on

My heart is like a shattered mirror!
I've just written down this run-of-the-mill colloquial expression and
        let me assure you that I think highly of kitsch.
Again I'm lying on the cushions of the divan.
It's dark, but there are no lights on in the room.
Through the twilit shadows the naked woman comes and goes.
Softly she steps, thinking me asleep, but
        I'm not asleep. I'm watching her through my eyelids,
spying on the naked movements of her naked body.
As the saying goes, the girl's a "hind," a "doe."
Now the naked woman is standing in front of the mirror and
        trying on a tiny black hat with a veil, adjusting it over and over.
I want to fuck that little filly again—of course,
        I prefer the word "filly" to "doe."
It's a Sunday morning, ten years ago, and
        I'm wandering through the Archaeological Museum of
        Athens.
In a remote display case an overturned coupe and
on the coupe this sacred scene:
        a couple is making love, and it's perfectly clear how
        the man sticks his prick up her rear.
In the ancient days of Greece nothing was pure white.
        I edge my way through the flock: a lot of ewes, a few
        she-goats.
        Their sheep bells, their goat bells jingle-jangle.
        The sheepdogs bark and I listen.

the fourth poem, with its wacky rhymes

In my land they all write serious poetry,
    but I prefer charlatans and to-and-froetry.
That's his mug I see in the mirror over there.
    The fishermen are shouting: "Ahoy! Ahoy there!"
The house is on fire, you're scratching your ass.
    She seizes the fan and beats the air fast.
Finally got a hard-on, I throw the smut aside.
    Give me the clothespins, I'll hang the wash outside.
Underneath the cypress is where they buried him,
    his daughter and his widow are crying over him.
The meditative sailor takes a fag from his pack;
    a yellow bird alights on the tall smokestack.
He jogs round the track every Sunday at four.
    He dislikes the landscape, so flat it's a bore.
The cat curled up on the living room chair.
    He ran into a rock, his nose in the air.
He slit his wife's throat, she was a harlot;
    got another wife now, her name is Charlotte.
He wasn't convinced though they used their wits;
    he lost his faith when they gave him the shits.
She's as fat as a hog, he digs her all the more;
    he just barely managed it; he bagged the whore.
A comb and a golden mirror she uses
    (one fucks and the other abuses),
artistically she parts her hair
    (a hole in front and a hole derriere).
        Family, Country, Flag and God,
        scabies, rabies, cholera and a cod.

..................In Berlin: Notebook 1983-1984........................

I don't believe at all in Inspiration.
I consider Poetry to be mere Gymnastic Exercise.
I'll have to write a Manifesto of Ugly Poetry.

The Freikorps and then the SS with the same skull and crossbones
The skull and crossbones everywhere and everlasting
                        from the armored cars of '19
                                to the Totenkopf Division.

In the history of photography
only one single ass exists,
the ass that Man Ray photographed in 1930
                        (its title is, I think, *Close-up*).

From my window I see Mariannenplatz.
It's October 30th and on a day like today
$\qquad$ (exactly thirty-nine years ago)
they killed my father
and we never found his body.
At least we missed out on the funeral and the graveyard procession.

You can see the whole world
through the eye of a needle;
just as you can see
$\qquad$ (yes, the whole world!)
through an asshole.

When I hear the word *culture* I draw my gun
$\qquad$ —said Mr. Hermann Goering
Today, in Berlin, culture is in a rage
$\qquad$ —once again.

Berlin-Museum, I adore you!
Martin-Gropius-Bau. The architecture! The paintings!
Prisons of Moabit
$\qquad$ (windowless prisons),
$\qquad$ you disgust me!

With friends in the Paris Bar.
To my right sits Hermann Nitsch and Ludmila
                          (a blonde with a shapely ass)
and to my left another German woman. Who,
                               a little drunk, she suggests:
—Shall we go to my place?
—I can't. That's my wife sitting over there. . .
And my wife asks me, in Greek:
—What's going on? She got a hold of your prick?
—Not yet. . .
Michel treats us to beers,
                speaking German, Italian, French, Greek.
Ossi Wiener chats with the President of Austria,
                    who happens to be in the room.
Someone asks:
—Is today December 21st?

Closed down forever, the Café Megalomania,
and homeless artists now take refuge
over there, around Savignyplatz,
or in AX-BAX, in Leibnizstrasse.

The Germans had a word, *Schick*,
but the French stole it
to make their own word, *chic*
             (the Latin word sic is another story),
and then the Germans took it back again
and forged the word *Schickeria*.
My friends tell me over and over:
—Don't hang around with the Berlin Schickeria.
And I always answer:
—But there are beautiful women in the Schickeria. . .

—What's that you got, sweetheart, between your thighs?
—Where?
—There. There!
—You mean my little pussy?

The immense, labyrinthine Headquarters
of the Wehrmacht General Staff
with those terrifying courtyards, one after another.
In one of those courtyards the Hitlerians liquidated several (until '44)
equally Hitlerian officers.
The Hitlerian von Stauffenberg, how he deserved it!
        —and France houses
                its General Consulate there?

It's December 27th
and I'm sitting in the Kneipe *Terzo Mondo*,
waiting for my wife.
I'm murmuring that Greek song which goes:
    Sleep took hold of me and I lay down in the prow of the ship
    and then the captain's daughter came and woke me...
At the next table a blonde is writing letters.

We were angry at each other again.
We slept ass to ass.

Every noon,
while going to pick up my mail
at the Bethanien office,
I always stop in the hallway and look
at the large drawing by Otto Dix
        with its supposedly fully-dressed women
                —who are even more naked than naked.

One snowy evening
at a theater in Kreuzberg,
watching *The Good Person of Szechwan*,
suddenly, without reason, I remembered Constantine
                (I mean our idiotic king)
who was kicked out of Greece
one winter night in '67.
That gift, so unexpected, came from the Junta,
and not, naturally, from the voting of the greasy Greeks.
        Nothing evil unmixed with good—said our forefathers.

Months ago in West Berlin
a group of demonstrators was brought to trial.
I scrutinized in the newspapers the photograph of the woman judge:
a real sweat hog,
        a *malbaisée*.

> *Riko-Riko-Ebiriko.*

I love a Greek poet
> (in my fatherland we have great poets)

who wrote only about pussies
and this same poet that I love
photographed, like a maniac, only pussies.
> *Riko-Riko-Ebiriko.*

Today the poet whom I'm talking about is dead
and his widow is responsible for seeing him honored:
so she won't publish the pussy-poems
> and has stashed away for good the lyrical pussy-photographs.
> *Riko-Riko-Ebiriko.*

Thus, our poet will remain eternal,
since he won't get into school textbooks.
> *Riko-Riko-Ebiriko.*

Even though I'm not an important poet
I do hope that my heirs
will not play the same dirty trick on me.
> *Riko-Riko-Ebirika!*

The Ente is a restaurant over there in Yorkstrasse:
                        pass under the bridge and you're there.
I think it's the best eating place in Berlin,
but its patrons are few.
Ente, in German, means *duck*.

I want to become a Model Citizen
and so (starting tomorrow)
I plan to keep the Twelve Commandments, faithfully.
Thus, among other things,
       I'll never fuck a butt again.
               I imagine that, in the end, I shall be decorated.

My balls are swollen.
The cause? *La littérature française.*
I'm sitting in a café on the Kudamm
and from a nearby table
hear people talking about Chateaubriand, about La Fontaine,
and about other little doodads
that France has been slipping us for centuries.

Ass-pear
>	women of the Middle East
>	and saggy-assed Greek ladies.

Ass-apple
>	gorgeous German ladies
>	clean and polished little chicks

Ass-apple, well
>	that's the one I like the best.

Once again I take the U-Bahn
to get off at Zoo
and once again I gaze at the passengers.
Widows, all of them widows, shit-hags,
the famous widows of Berlin
with their ridiculous hats.
All these shit-hags, prick-bags, all of them
>	vote for the Right Wing and tip off the police by telephone.

They all worked for Hitler
>	nurses, workers, easy lays. . .

They show you the Wall and whisper:
>	—On this side, Freedom!
>	—On the other side, Terrorism!
>	(American propaganda works like a clock.)

I photograph your graffiti:
>	TÜRKEN RAUS. . . JUDEN RAUS. . .
>	Whose Freedom are you talking about, hypocrites?

In Paris, women walking
                    click their heels and shake their tails.
Brawny German women don't need heels.
On the sidewalks of Berlin are never heard
                              heels; that is, women's heels.

I'm a worthless piece of shit and
                    (because of what I am)
West Berlin suits me fine.
Drowsy Paris doesn't.
I already feel homesick for Berlin and I haven't left yet.

All day long I walked amidst the gravestones
in the Jewish Cemetery on Schönhauser Allee.
                              I wept like a little child. . .

I want to reminisce;
you're talking, you're asking me something,
you won't leave me alone so I can reminisce
and I want to rem-in-isce,
about how that night in '44 we barely escaped
the Germans who were tracking us down,
shooting at us with their submachine guns
          (—that's right, we too unleashed a hand grenade,
          that's how we must have escaped. . .)
I have grown old and it does me good to reminisce,
          —but you, now you're asking me something again. . .

Whoever has not lived through a New Year's Eve
                            in West Berlin
          doesn't know anything about New Year's Eves.
At one o'clock firecrackers and skyrockets are shot off,
          which cost, it is said, two million marks.
I left the ball for the sidewalk
          to enjoy the colors and the noise,
          but then, afraid, went back in;
          and it was freezing cold outside.
An old hag of a fag, dressed like a First World War aviator.
Ossi Wiener had vanished somewhere.
Fritz Gilow, completely plastered, came staggering in and
shouted: *Viva il Culo!*
Gizela and Mary dragged him out.
Thoroughly exhausted, I sat down on the couch.

Dammit!
I came to Berlin without
my beautiful edition of Casanova's *Memoirs*.
Luckily I didn't forget Thoreau's *Walden*
and *The Iliad*.
   —my three favorite books.

Unforgettable *Fassuliasuppe*!
Steaming hot bean soup in a Turkish greasy-spoon
         —bean soup and bread four marks.
And then to hear Senih
playing Ottoman taxims on his fiddle.
            —ah, quit shitting on me with your Bach.
            I'm already sick and tired of him. . .

I take a taxi to Herbert-Baum-Strasse,
     where the other large Jewish Cemetery is still located.
I wander around for hours. I take pictures.
                There's the grave of the Tucholsky family.
                And there's the grave of a soldier from the Red Army.

I'm already sure of it: Berlin is
the most interesting city in Europe;
      or rather, the Heart of Europe.

The Great Napoleon was a little runt;
    this, everyone knows.
The Great Napoleon had a little wiener;
    this, the autopsy report,
        written by caustic Englishmen, shows.
But French assholes avoid talking about such matters.
They prefer to say (with secret pride) that
      Bonaparte, as soon as he had taken a woman aside,
        sprung upon her the famous *déshabillez-vous!*
I detest Psychoanalysis, but I would like to learn why,
    because of that incompetent dung heap of a good-for-nothing,
        Europe ended up covered with carcasses.
If at least he had been a competent field marshal...

February 8th
    and a light snow is falling.
From my window I see the square
    and I'll stay inside.

I've heard it said that Adam and Eve
didn't have navels.
Angels were sexless as well,
but they did have nice round asses.
I asked a Spanish professor:
—In his *Ode to Walt Whitman*,
            what the devil ticked off Lorca into insulting pansies?
—Don't you know that Lorca was a cowardly closet queen,
        like your own Yiannis Ritsos?"
—In Italy *finocchio* always means *queer*,
        but what does *finocchio* mean literally?"
—*Finocchio* means *fennel* and, in the old days,
        when queers were burned on public squares,
        bundles of fennel were thrown into the blaze
        so that the roasting flesh wouldn't stink so much. . .
—So why didn't they use aromatic herbs
            in the ovens of Buchenwald?

Ah, this Berlin atmosphere!
Ah, this Berlin melancholy!

Reinsch explains:
—There, into that canal, they threw
              Rosa Luxemburg and Karl Liebknecht;
                    that is, they threw their corpses.
I look on with curiosity. I see nothing strange.
The cars glide by.
It is snowing. The canal is not frozen over.

I'm back in the synagogue.
The democratic nature of the service impresses me.
I listen and watch.

Today, since it's a Sunday serene,
>I'm going to write an "Ode to Saint Vaseline."
—Don't even say that as a joke,
or at holy mass you're taking a poke.
—Hey, the service is going to debut
with one helluva screw.
>Whereupon
I baptize my prick with green aniline
and then I smear it with Vaseline.
>She, however,
having chafed her hands washing dishes,
is advised by me, with secret wishes:
—Hey, Julie, that sweet talk, cut it out.
Just get the old Nivea out.
—Nivea, Nivea, and lanoline
or perhaps you'd like that old standby, Vaseline?
—Über alles Vaseline,
especially when on an ass I'm keen.
—That Vaseline has stained my sheets again. . ."
"The same thing happened to the wife of Ken."

The Tunisian artist Messaoud Chebbi
>has been living in Germany for ten years.
The Polizei was searching for him
so at Easter
we organized an exhibition in protest.
I exhibited a collage:
>a Jewish chick from Auschwitz
>and above her the caption
>À BAS LA NOUVELLE GESTAPO!

Don't you know, my little Gudrun,
             who the Blitzmädchen were?
That is, didn't they tell you at school?
             Didn't you ever read anything about them? . . .
Well, listen carefully, my little dear.
The Blitzmädchen were those big blond cunts
             that only Wehrmacht officers were allowed to fuck.
I'm speaking about the Second World War,
             when brothels with Blitzmädchen
                  were located in all the cities of occupied Europe.
The Blitzmädchen dressed like soldiers:
      a garrison cap, a gray jacket, a short skirt, a pair of bluchers with
      two-inch heels.
Whenever a Blitzmädchen got pregnant,
      they would send her to Bavaria to have the baby;
      afterwards, it was taken from her, forever.
They say that in Germany today
             about a half million such bastard children live—so they say.
Blitzmädchen means *Thunderbolt Girl.*
Gudrun, I heard that your mom was one of those Blitzmädchen.

Whenever a couple mounts a staircase,
of necessity shall the male escort proceed,
whereupon the female
             as the Book of Etiquette stipulates
                  (without explaining why).
I'm no imbecile.
I always go up stairs
      and follow the female
             so I can observe her buttocks.

At the Plötzensee Martyrium
they give you a 32-page booklet
which mostly describes the Germans' so-called *resistance*
    to Hitlerism.
it is a despicable, Neo-Nazi text.

I enter the Treptow Cemetery with awe:
    here, here, and in Pankow, and in Marzahn,
        are buried thousands of soldiers from the Red Army.
I contemplate the mound over the mass grave
    so as not to forget the Post-Nazi Mythology:
        —*The Russians eat toothpaste!*
        —*The Russians rape German women!*
Swine, I like the Russians,
and I know that thanks to the Red Army we survived,
and I refuse to forget the crimes of the Wehrmacht,
and I'm glad, I'm very glad,
that the venerable Soviet Memorial
    is stuck right in the heart of West Berlin,
and I will sleep soundly
as long as that Soviet Memorial exists, there, in the Tiergarten.
Only in your pseudo-democratic country did I understand the slogan:
    Better red than dead.

Hubert Selby, Jr., that horny stud,
is an asshole monomaniac.
I read his novel *The Room*
    and that sufficed.

Build your poem like a house is built.
Force yourself to write poems,
           even on days when you don't want to write poems.
Define, from the start, the form and content of the verses.
Concoct poems while playing.
Throw away the Poetry of Ideas and of Symbols and of Colors.
Prefer Everyday Images
           and insignificant Snapshots, one after another;
                      that is, Poor Poetry.
Goodbye Ginsberg, you old geezer!

I cross the new bridge
to enter the Citadel of Spandau.
The new railing of the bridge is decorated
with a series of military helmets.
The Hitlerian helmet is not missing.

Why was Stalin so nice
to the Germans?

I dream:
I am in a Kneipe
and she is drinking at the bar
              (because it's cheaper there)
and she is wearing black lamé pants
and as she sits down on the high barstool
her buttocks fan out
and I, like a cat, approach on the sly,
on tiptoe,
and reach out my hands
              to fondle her. . .

With a German friend I took a drive in East Berlin.
We ate somewhere before reaching Köpenick
and then continued southeast, towards Neu-Zittau.
We illegally left the city limits
and were, from then on, in the German Democratic Republic.
We passed in front of a Russian division
and saw the sentry looking us over suspiciously.
              —Armin, please, let's head for Erkner,
                  let's go back, I'm really afraid,
                      let's not chance our luck. . .
A half hour later we reached Friedrichshagen,
the historical summer resort of German anarchists.

Tsoclis confided in me
that he was painting couples fucking and the like.
But why won't he show his paintings to me?

Pankow, the end of the U-Bahn line,
and then a hike, an endless hike,
      I go through working-class neighborhoods and a small woods
and reach the other unknown cemetery of the Red Army
and from there head towards Rosenthal,
      where I photograph gravestones and leave.
To my left the *Wall of Shame*
      (as sold-out hack journalists have christened it),
           but I'm looking at it from the interior and walk alongside
and the sentries watch me with curiosity
and again I look at my map
      (—so that's Blankenfelde in front of me?)
and at once I photograph the knoll of the cemetery
and enter Blankenfelde,
and leave the village, towards the side of the little train station,
         heading for the Wall,
           but before reaching it the dogs are upon me
      and behind the dogs come running a terror-stricken soldier
         (to save me from the fangs of the dogs)
and in the end I am retained
and from the little building of the old train station
         comes a young officer
and he is extremely polite
         (they are all extremely polite)
and he tells me to wait.
Exhausted, I sit down on the grass
      while the officer goes into the little building to telephone.
And in two seconds he comes back out and says:
—Here's your passport,
      you can go back towards the village and
         photograph whatever you wish.
—Danke schön! Auf Widersehen!
And I start out for Schönerlinde,
    still walking, and I feel very, very tired
        and that blasted Schönerlinde is so far
           and, moreover, outside the Berlin city limits.
And, thinking it over, I hesitate,
        and in the end take the road to Buchholz
because how can I explain to Communists
      what I am doing in their cemeteries?

Kneeling over the bed
with her cheek on a pillow
and her ass flung up,
with her ass in the air,
an ideal pose for a photograph.
      Of course, the woman is completely naked.

Once again I go to the Soviet Memorial.
Unwillingly I smile:
—Hey Germans, now you're paying for all those *Alles kaputt's*
      Wehrmacht soldiers said when
           with voluptuous discipline they were liquidating us. . .

—I'll fuck your eyes
—Can it be done?
—I want to shave your pussy with a Gillette razor.
—Why?
—I'll be fucking you and taking photographs.
—You like doing that?
—I'll be giving it to you for a blowjob
      until all your teeth rot away.
—But since I don't swallow the come. . .
—Your little pussy will open out like a carnation.
—Come closer. Right here beside me.

On Fridays I go to the synagogue,
                        Pestalozzistrasse 14.
The cantor is from Salonica
and I like listening to him chanting.
His name is Estrongo Nachama.
He has never spoken to me about Thessaloniki.
He must be very bitter about the past.

West Berlin, Steinplatz.
Memorial No. 1, for the Victims of Nazism.
Memorial No. 2, for the Victims of Communism.
            Quel culot!

Kudamm, Kudamm,
with your sidewalk showcases,
with your sluts
       qui font boutique de leur cul.
Every ten meters, a showcase.
Every showcase, a slut.

            These past nights I've been dreaming
            of all my friends who were shot dead.

................................Letter to A. Kanavakis................................

I possess the Woman's Body and this is how the Woman possesses me.
We must face up to Erotic Faithfulness as the
                                      hypocritical form par excellence
                    of permanent Physical Occupation.
You always want to devour the Woman-Whom-You-Worship.
Contemporary Pornography
                    is but the Romanticism of our Times.
Aretino rightly didn't want to understand why it is bad
              to see a Man riding a Woman.
We consider an Erotic Complex to be an abominable sculpture.
The *Kama Sutra* classifies Erotic Positions
                in a strictly geometric manner.
Eros is not a symptom of esteem.
The Prostitute provides Love as the Absolute Good;
          the Prostitute is rewarded with a Relative Good
                            —that is, with Money.
Penal Codes include dozens of anti-erotic articles.
The Avenue of Phalluses was the main street of Delos.

      According to the old saying,
      Beauty uses the Devil's Ass as a Mirror.

The Woman I see walking on the sidewalk
                                  is desirable.
Christianity taught us how
                          we glorify Shit with the Sexual Act.
A Naked Woman shines even brighter than the Sun.
Christian iconography,
                in order to give us a peek at the Virgin's Bosom,
          resorted to the pretext of breastfeeding the Divine Infant.
Obviously, the Virgin is not Aphrodite's daughter.
Neither Aphrodite nor Priapus
                              were Greek deities.
Pornography is distinguished by its limited,
                            extremely small vocabulary.
Paganism emerges from within Eroticism.
Casanova wrote what Félicien Rops will see.

It's very likely that we are facing a New Renaissance.
The sex shop turns out to be more necessary and indispensable
                                       than the neighborhood grocery store.
Erotic posters are on the walls of Paris
                                       —and they sigh.
Let's cut the bread into small pieces
                             so that everyone can fuck.
However, no kind of Communism will succeed (no it won't)
                                       in reducing Erotic Inequality:
the Village Hunchback will not enjoy the Beautiful Woman.
We are drifting, all the time we are gently drifting
                               towards a New Erotic Religion.
When you're in the Labyrinth you don't see the Labyrinth.

    Oh, Satan Trismegistus,
    come back to help Human Beings!

Caricature bites like a wasp and flees elsewhere.
You give me *The Brothers Karamazov* to read,
                              but I prefer Crepax's albums.
With true Wisdom you exorcise Nightmares.
She, that Erotic Girl,
the one mounted on the Erotic Bicycle, crosses
                                    (the golden-haired wind)
              the curved bridges of Amsterdam.
The Naked Woman, beautiful as the Moon,
                    more glorious than the Glory of Heaven.
In Red China, issues of *Playboy*
        have a more stable monetary value than the local currency.
Painters, with their snobbery, pretend not to see
                          comics and graphic novels,
           nor Haute Couture fashion designers.
A well-fitting pair of female panties
                is as dynamic as a Maserati.
Tom Wesselmann opens the Door of Desire.
Only Eroticism can stop
                    the possible Nuclear Disaster.

..............................**Inaccessible Tsoclis**..............................

Only after looking at Tsoclis's works did I discover why
the scaffolding around a building site is so beautiful
The horizon stands out horizontally haltingly haltingly—
Tsoclis cuts the painted landscape with clusters of verticals
I'd again like to speak about olives and herds however
but the airplanes are buzzing potently
I don't like lines of verse since I like style
Tsoclis slides inside his own personal moment
I am free means I am expecting
waiting for my own moment

Tsoclis had to give me a shove so I could see for the first time
so I could sense the nostalgia given off by iron rods
I delight in walking across Paris with Tsoclis because
he has a steady step
The Moon and the Sea are objects of great nobility
rightly deified along with Tsoclis
Tsoclis has used many everyday objects
as substitutes for imposing deities
Art disarms Thought
Every elevation of a trivial object to the Mythic level
demands Seven Thousand Years and thus begins to dazzle
Tsoclis writes to me of course
the field of Art cannot be penetrated by the Intellect but
I believe that even this could happen
The significance of methodology is minor and mechanistic
I bought a new pair of eyes to approach Tsoclis then
I saw only then I saw that he had nailed the Moon to the wall

Tsoclis arrives with a diagonal and he—
he Rightly kills us with a diagonal
Rightly I end up thinking that in his work the—
the oblique tension expresses revolt
and that even that
the diagonal appears as a subversive presence as—
as disturbing energy and so on
The Moon is compressed into a round mirror
and the boat sails flap like flags
A boulder came unstuck from Tsoclis's painting
and the rock rolled down to my feet
like something in excess or some extract of the painted landscape
I draw from this the lesson that arbitrariness if it happens
along with inaccessible simplicity announces calm
The Painter re-creates reality by stepping over the Magician
painter is a geometer equal to God
I love Tsoclis for his harshness especially
when he peacefully peels away monotonous tenderness
Brevity is the sister of talent said
sighed and said Chekhov

I saw Tsoclis's *Medea* in Troyes France
and thus recalled Homeric Troy Whenever
historical History is elevated to mythic Mythology
the vultures attack and tear the ancient purple
Only little children daydream as they listen to Myths since
because a Myth hides no meaning nor
either does a Myth symbolize
With his *Medea* Tsoclis came in discreetly
I roamed in the dark tight circle of the Myth
The Nations of the World put to use several Myths about Bread
The modest Tomato hasn't managed to sneak
into Greek Mythology—it would be odd and like going backwards
Tsoclis built his own optic Myth on the written *Medea*
The ancient Greeks served Myths without sauce And
in the same way depicted them and
we will never know why they painted them on vases
(those celestial vases full of oil or wine)
which were simply sold to distant peoples therefore
to foreigners who understood neither the painted scenes
nor the Greek names full of spelling mistakes
written from right to left or in the other direction
Tsoclis's mute *Medea* has its foundations
in a half-dark atmosphere of sacred awe
The sociologists the historians the literati have run off and vanished
—they are the vultures I was speaking of

In Troyes I drank a big black German beer
and as darkness was falling I went into the church to—
where I watched *Medea* being shown
since it was of course a film projection that's what it was
And I saw the video-film with wide-open eyes
and I saw it with my logic locked up
And I said exactly this to Tsoclis and he retorted
> *you saw Medea as a film whereas I presented*
> *presented a sequence of alternating images*
> *images that each had its own value*
> *images simply linked to each other by movement*

I think *Damn!* this and
only this is the definition of cinema
I demand the Spectator's Freedom for myself
and I will see the Work of Art however I want
> And this is why I shout down *any doctrine formulated by Artists!*

Thought penetrates neither Myth nor Art
I have no intention of submitting myself to Theory and Method
Myth is hermetic And Art is hermetic
I've read all the theories of Myths all of them
were nothing but rotten potatoes
I give the deathblow to Levi-Strauss's books
who grew old trying to comprehend
what he should have sensed and smelled
The Mind must first seize with force
and then the Heart feel the warmth of what the Mind has grasped
the famous phrase of the Greek-Jewish poet Salomon
stinks of classical German philosophy
Tsoclis's *Medea* is like a clock being wound up
while no one wants to wind it up
Medea evolves freely over unfastened time
I have a myriad of reasons to admire Tsoclis
and I found another myriad that night
in the church that night I watched the video-film
A joyous dinner followed the projection
to prove that we were walking firmly on the earth

Tsoclis dressed Medea like a queen
Queens don't slaughter children but
anguished I watched the bright red blood trickling
flowing into a colorful crescendo
                         and slowly crowning the Impious Deed
This I offer as a compliment.
From the holy ceremonial Slaughter were missing
did not appear at all (as Tsoclis intended)
                         the Knives and the innocent young Victims
Tsoclis trusted the magic of suggestiveness
This is my second compliment

Tsoclis telephoned me
I often prefer objects to paintings
because it is emotion that interests me
wherever the emotion comes from
Assuming that he used the word *objects*
I recalled courteously and respectfully
came back to mind those human Shadows
the silent visions in *Medea*
progressing imperceptibly in slow motion
since they had been dead for many centuries
and with them the Heroes and Demigods of the Heroic Age
and that funeral procession in *Medea*
confirmed for me Tsoclis's cool lyric majesty
When the image of death is pale and vague
it frightens us less
The slow motion of the Dead Souls which we discover
for the first time in Homer's *Nekyia*
I'm always frightened when I read the eleventh rhapsody of *The Odyssey*
I suspect that Tsoclis manages to compel Inspiration

I'm sitting in my study with Tsoclis
and we're chatting about his enchanting dreams
He has taken a photo of his latest dream and I look at it
It's Saint George astride his horse
as he stabs sideways with incredible indifference
he kills the Dragon with his lance
and the lance is a murderous diagonal
        a diagonal that goes crazy and leaps out of the painting
For us Greeks Saint George on his gray
and Saint Demetrios on his chestnut horse
are two beloved figures of Orthodox iconography
I ask Tsoclis how he fashions the Reptile's scales
and he explains *from cast metal* and then
later I say to myself that *this Saint George looks like*
                seems to me to be a Centaur
Tsoclis partly agrees because it offers him
the right and the freedom
to make out many other things behind the Serpent
behind Saint George the Horse Rider
I didn't say that *Saint George is a Centaur*
Saint George looks like a Centaur is what I said
        All equestrian statues play the role of Centaurs

These discussions with Tsoclis all our disagreements
are but monologuing dialogues
which in retrospect constantly influence me
which compel me to go back to his work
You sense Tsoclis better when you muse when you think about
the diabolical Subversions which he has already meted out on us
and in which we already delight as in ruby-colored wine
I consider that the axis of my discussions with Tsoclis are
the meaning of his Talent and
the meaning of Revolution in Art
which is to say the comparison between a Rose and
an unhesitant Bulldozer
The skillful artist gives us paintings of great beauty
and we love him because he caresses us But the Other One
the revolutionary artist opens the road
and frightens us and infuriates us and eats away at our guts
and we accept him only when he has conquered us
Tsoclis tames our ignorance
My gratitude is the tiniest gift that I can give him
And in addition
      I send him the heartfelt greetings
      every Dear Friend deserves

..........................An Encomium to Cicciolina..........................

The former Prime Minister of Italy described Cicciolina as a *sinister phenomenon*. Vulgarity usually takes off its panties, whereas Hypocrisy always wears something—at least a fig leaf. Modestly responding to the prime minister, Fellini said: *Cicciolina is every Italian man's secret dream*. The bourgeoisie agrees to discuss Phyrne's trial, but not Cicciolina's breasts. Beauty, the Beauty of the Body, is the Absolute Value. And the ancient Greeks, as well as the modern Greeks, knew this magnificently well. Hypocrisy is the insignificant virtue that opposes Vulgarity. I do not consider Cicciolina to be a representative of (already dead) feminism. I prefer to see her as a flower, as an antelope, as a butterfly. Vulgarity provides me with a framework of comfort. The Hypocrite is especially annoyed by the so-called legitimacy of the Naked Body. According to one of Spinoza's theorems, we can only have an extremely imperfect knowledge of how long our body will last. The Naked Body does not reflect my feelings. The Naked Body imposes feelings on me. The two extreme ways of exorcising the Body are either by covering it up or by exposing it. In classical Athens, some three thousand statues of naked men and naked women were erected. The Greeks were rightly afraid of clothed people. Christianity, on the other hand, fought with rage until the Naked Body disappeared or, at least, was identified with Sin. Ultimately, the Naked Body triumphed again in Painting and in Sculpture and in Poetry. Islam has followed the dark path: the tattered niqab deforms the female body and the yashmak hides facial expressions. The mask of the Carnival of Venice was worn almost all year round. The great Aretino wished that women could have their cunt on their forehead. Every Naked Woman shines in her glory. Cicciolina wears the crown of her own glory.

Our century opens with the miserable ideas of Marx and Freud and closes, majestically, with Pornography. Specialists vainly seek to define the difference between Eroticism and Pornography. Definitions have a great attraction for academics. The word *vagina* begins with a V (like *victory*). Marx was in no mood to talk about obscene matters. The road from Balzac's novels to Rops' *Pornocratès* is difficult. In the work of sullen Freud you do not find the slightest trace of humor. I am always impressed by Cicciolina's shy grace. Of course, there are many kinds of Vulgarities (e.g., unintentional, popular, provocative, necessary, pornographic), but the Vulgarity of Hypocrisy is itself so self-evident that, in the end, we do not see it. Hypocrisy is the supreme vileness; it is the Vulgarity of the Worthless. The Hypocrite sees and knows and remains silent. I occasionally see one of Rembrandt's engravings (inspired by Callot's similar designs, a fact that Jacques Sternberg ignores), showing a peasant woman *faisant ses besoins* ("relieving herself")—this is the ultimate caption of the work, because there used to be more modest ones. That is, it took almost four centuries for museum curators to confess, convolutedly, that Rembrandt had drawn a woman peeing after having taken a shit. It is easier for the Hypocrite to throw mud at Cicciolina than to talk seriously about the asshole. Proctology hasn't even managed to enter the field of Medicine. In the voluminous and authoritative *Medicine: An Illustrated History*, by Albert S. Lyons / R. Joseph Petrucelli, New York, 1978), I could not find the words *anus / clyster / enema / rectum*, etc., even as I did not come across other such words in the *Lexicon der Liebe* (1984) by the rather shy Ernest Borneman. Moralistic scientists are bad scientists. Europeans are screaming about censorship in various *foreign countries* (which, precisely because of Europeans, are under dictatorial regimes) because they do not realize that open censorship is milder (and I would say, more beneficial) than the unbearable Terror of the Press, as we see it and experience it in Europe. The bourgeoisie accepted Pornography only after it had become a source of profit. Casanova slipped into the shadows during the period 1830-1930, when comments about his *Mémoires* (that is, that Novel of the Centuries) were whispered around. Today, Casanova is still a bird locked up in a golden cage—to have him sing you have to slip 1500 francs to the publisher. This is why the Beast roars. The Beast is called the Devil. In Anatolia, hand-kissing began as foot-kissing. Inferiors would humbly kiss the feet (or the hem of the gown) of the king and the high priest, without glancing at his face. Byzantine and Arabic protocol gave some minor nobles and officials the privilege of kissing the hand of the king, or the clergy (—hypocrisy and second-class slavery). In today's Greece, the faithful continue to kiss the hand of Orthodox priests (—traditional hypocrisy). Foot-kissing and archaic hand-kissing therefore signified submission among men in male-dominated societies. The hand-kissing that nobles and gallants practiced with women seems to have been born (like many other things) in Italy, from where it took root in the French Court. When an old woman offers me her hand for a kiss, I want to bite it. However, I would kiss Cicciolina's hands with passion. The Devil attends to His chosen ones: Aretino, Boccaccio, Rops, Topor and Arrabal, Buñuel, Mac Orlan, Courbet, Bosch and Breughel the Elder, Schiele, Kubin, Otto Dix, Goya, Fellini, Paul Delvaux (he's not French), Aat Veldhoen, George Grosz. The Devil is not content with halfway measures because He demands that they kiss His asshole even when He takes on the form of a Goat. I think this is a small price to pay for the royal gifts that the Devil gives to His favorites.

Oppressive Hypocrisy induces, every time, an explosion of Profanity. British Hypocrisy resulted in the unforgettable Beatles. I consider Roland Topor to be a consistent outburst against Parisian Hypocrisy. According to one of Plato's poems, Lais, the aged Lais, offered her mirror to Aphrodite because she could no longer bear to see her withered face. In the struggle, lost in advance, of a Beautiful Woman against Time, Hypocrisy is inserted, very annoyingly. Many have been convicted of Vulgarity—no one of Hypocrisy. The Hypocrite claims that Vulgarity stinks. At the Berlin Museum in 1983, I was introduced to a serene exhibition on the traditional homosexuality of German officers. Vulgarity has the aroma of rotten apple. Diogenes the Cynic masturbated in front of his big jar, thus showing (publicly) his preference for Vulgarity over Hypocrisy. The Vulgar person is not provocative enough. The Vulgar person sees the First Anarchist in Diogenes's face, whereas the Hypocrite considers him to be a bum. When Cicciolina grabs her breast, she offers us a tin can of Pleasure: it is the only role that our ruthless Society allows her. This is why Cicciolina's presence in the European Parliament sparked waves of outrage. I hope to find some answers to the duality of Vulgarity / Hypocrisy in G. Legman's memoirs. It is better to accommodate yourself with the Devil whom you hide, deep down, in your soul.

I'm delighted to return to the ass and the asshole. My persistence is not due to aesthetic extremism, but because the asshole remains the eternal taboo. And we do not know exactly why the asshole is taboo. I dislike arguments. I love color. Arguments are addressed to the mind, but the mind is an imperfect instrument. Our skin thinks much better than the mind. However, Praxiteles's Hermes is crammed into a corner of the Museum of Olympia, so that his ass is not visible—that is, the most sensual detail of this statue. All the visitors of the Museum of Delphi, feeling the invincible need to caress the ass of the statue depicting Antinous, push themselves with some difficulty behind the marble teenager from Bithynia. Antinous had driven Hadrian crazy, but the director of the Museum of Delphi did not seem to share the vulgar tastes of the Roman emperor. The first postcard showing the ass of Aphrodite of Milos was printed just three years ago—and in this way was discovered, after the far side of the Moon, the backside of the much-publicized statue of the Louvre. A sense of modesty as regards the asshole can also appear in the case of tortures. Ivo Andrič described in detail how impalement took place during the Ottoman Empire. I think that I saw the best picture of this terrible martyrdom in a French magazine from 1876. However, it is noteworthy that the executioner gradually (with great care) plunged the sharp stick into the convict's asshole without stripping him naked. Thus, the voracious Crowd could watch the free spectacle, with the certainty that state Hypocrisy would not revel in popular Vulgarity. Tortures had their own Law of Aesthetics. This is also the case with the charming custom of Persia, where the husband skinned his unfaithful wife and nailed her skin to the wall, so that relatives and neighbors could see it. The unfaithful flayed woman would remain alive for a few more hours and also look at it. Some Catholics would happily flay Cicciolina as well.

It is impossible to form a system of relations between the conflicting and complementary forces of Vulgarity and Hypocrisy. The Vulgar Person is not a criminal. The Vulgar Person wears his socks inside out. Vulgarity is almost always revolutionary. You often discover Hypocrisy hidden behind a false bravery—here I refer to the novel *The Name of the Rose*, which I consider to be a well-made book, but skillfully hypocritical. Umberto Eco worked for the Vatican and that is the secret of his book's commercial success. In Vulgarity, a Pattern, a Target, a Purpose can be made out halfway. Cicciolina must have an angelic soul—this, at least, is shown by her smile.

..........................Four Seasons: Roland Topor..........................

Topor Winter

Saturday evening. I hurry down the rue de Seine
(the market is still open)
to reach, as usual, La Palette—and
I go inside; Abram is already seated at his place.
I assure you, on my honor, that
what I'm writing here is a poem, a ser—
serious poem about Topor's Art,
but for the moment, as I drink a blond beer,
I instead feel like whipping off a little song:
>   *Why go an' eat another tomato*
>   *When you're already fat like a potato*

Topor, reading over my shoulder, cuts in:
—You might have written about my Lofty Aspirations, no?
—Ah, Topor, you're that Minotaur who,
indeed, doesn't like highfalutin words.
Our friends are drinking elbow to elbow at the bar.
Jacques Vallet is whispering something to Olivier, the painter.

Arslan, hiding behind his moustache, is chatting in Turkish
with Komet and Selçuk.
Perhaps it's raining outside.
A waiter shouts his way through the crowd.
There are lots of people around me but I withdraw,
close myself up,
vaguely listening to Topor laughing.
Yes, I know, above all I come to La Palette
to see Topor.
Absently, I play with small change in my hand,
stare at the franc. It shows Mme Liberté in relief
encircled by the words *C'est discret!*
I look at a twenty-centime coin with Mlle Marianne's profile
crowned with the inevitable *C'est gentil!*
Outraged, I examine the new 10-franc coin—
a winged Hermes, about to fly off,
farting on the exclamation of French diplomacy: *Prudence!*
In Paris, Hypocrisy has always circulated like money.
How does this country manage to survive Topor's dagger stabs?

Topor Spring

Topor's women have come, come running,
tossing away their panties and coming in naked,
with their cackling little laughs and their asses stuck out.
Spring, and sunlight, and Parisiennes passing by.
Let me repeat: a sunlit Paris is
a glorious city it is
a sunlit Paris it is another Paris.
As a child I learned to admire naturally,
without thinking, Gustave Doré's engravings.
Topor (fortunately) is undecipherable and
I have never tried to find his secret code.
Trees begin to bud because—
Sitting on the wicker chairs in front of La Palette,
we observe women's legs.
Buds and legs—optimistic signs.
Let the glasses on the table wait
for smiling Otsuki, who arrives wearing a turban.

A girl comes near and Topor leaps up
to embrace her with the traditional triple kiss.
Fellini claims to be fascinated by immense melancholy—
Topor's, of course.
I spot Roman Cieslewicz at the back of the café
and hurry over to him, respectfully—Maître (I say),
do you prefer the Parthenon or the Cathedral of Chartres?
—I prefer apples to pears (he doesn't reply).
Topor's answers refer to the Great Fear
and he indeed intended that, when he wrote in '65:
La seule revolte individuelle consiste à survivre.
The more one nears the Quai de Conti, the more the rue de Seine
narrows, and this is why the cars are moving along sluggishly. I stare at them.
Let critics write criticism. It's commonplace to point out
Topor's anxiety, Topor's monomanias, Topor's shits.
Through Topor's writing and drawing, Joy surges forth,
the Joy of Being Alive, and this strikes me as being his most significant quality.
I would simply like to show that Topor is a Good Man.
At the little table across from us the Devil is sitting alone and—
It's the first time that I've seen the Devil wearing a hat.

Topor Summer

This summer, the heat has been unbearable.
I'd like to know what Topor thinks of Félicien Rops
whom the French have not managed to appropriate, as
they've succeeded in doing for so many other Belgians.
I never miss an opportunity of seeing *Viva la Muerte*
(it should be shown in all schools)
and, well, Topor once told me
that the drawing he had made for Arrabal's film
had been stolen in New York.
And I climb the stairs to Topor's apartment
because the wooden staircase of his building is very beautiful
and reminds me of staircases I saw in Berlin
[While I'm writing, my telephone rings:
—I'd like to speak to Mlle Marguerite Duras.
—No, you've dialed the wrong number!]
After all, I hope I have the right
to suspect Topor of being an ardent feminist.

The only piece of furniture that Topor draws is a bed.
Obviously, he sees it as the Key of Dreams, rather than
a Tool of Voluptuousness covered with white sheets.
All right, all right,
Isaac Babel was a considerable writer but
at this moment I want to speak about the adventures of Tarzan.
Hole.
Someone next to me whispers: Those toothy pussies
that Topor draws look like—
I find them nightmarish and I'm afraid of them because.
And
(even if my nightmare is the architectural turd
called L'église de Saint-Sulpice)
I think that it's better
to have your prick bit by the Vagina Dentata
than by the venomous vipers of the Bourgeoisie.
I am overwhelmed by the heat.
Hole.
And because you insist: a flowery hole.
Despite the heat, I want to take revenge on my neighbor
who claims to be afraid of toothy pussies.
I thus explain to him that the Romans called this nightmare "Lamia"
and that this Lamia looked like a big snake with a woman's face.
Even today, Lamia silently sucks the—
feeds on the sperm of snoring men.
Topor's nightmares are perfectly legitimate.

Autumn Autumn

Autumn is the ideal season for suicide.
Topor wants to kill himself now (*parce que
c'est une bonne façon de m'arrêter de fumer*),
but this *spettacolo* is forbidden at La Palette.
Topor draws his gun like a cowboy.
I'm forced to take it from him. I give it to the barman.
I talk Topor into drawing a self-portrait because
egocentrism is considered to be an excellent antidote
against suicide.
Ah, this damned hole.
There are five of us around the table and five more
around us.
Most of them are already at their third glass,
while Dino is happy with a cup of warm tea.
Topor holds his glass with his left hand,
tracing small figures with his right hand.
I stick my finger in the glass of beer

and lick it.
Dino knows how to draw beautiful hands.
The man next to me turns and says: — Yesterday,
or the day before yesterday, I saw Topor in the street with a red tie.
I thought: Topor and a tie! Incompatible things!
In front of the *pipi-room*, two women are standing.
It's raining. I think I'll take refuge in a cinema tonight.

..........................**Never and Nothing**..............................

You ask me
—why are you so harsh?
I answer:
—out of tenderness.

At the café on the little square
and I'm waiting
for Jordan Plevnes to come down from his apartment.
Near me, a withered beauty is reading a book
(or, rather, pretending to read).
Her skin has begun to wrinkle
like old parchment.
This blasted sadness!

Twenty-five years have gone by since we separated.
I don't want to see you again,
I don't want to face
the ruins of your beauty.
Phryne should die at the height of her glory.

Down the avenue tomorrow the car
was streaking like mad,
seeking their suicide.
Grammarians can't stand errors
because they hate diction that vibrates.
I'm standing in front the green house.
It's drizzling.
You come close holding your red umbrella.
I fuck the grammar all you grammarians use!

That woman who turns her back on you,
let her go.
Sometimes the torment of separation
is preferable
to a presence that kills.

Rubens worked hard
to show us the beauty
of a fleshy woman,
because he spotted in her cellulite
the privilege of a Beautiful Race.
French women have a penchant
for puny lovers.
Believe me,
a big ass has what it takes
to delight the most difficult dick.
I understand very well why little farm boys
fuck cows and goats.

My friend Rodriguez Najar
wrote a beautiful poem about pussy lips.
And now here you are,
bent over the bed,
slipping your right hand down
and with your two fingers
you open your pussy lips,
while you look me straight in the eyes and nod.
Woe to the man who has never seen
the mouth of a Woman with her pussy lips
and with those lips in his mouth.

Love is an elastic passion.
Love is liquid
—and liquids cannot be restrained.

I like Moravia because of his writings.
But I also like him because he always wore
very beautiful ties.

I once again spent this year's Mayday
away from Paris,
at the house of Philolaos the sculptor.
I drink a little, I eat a little,
I speak a little with people nearby.
However, above all, I look around.
I watch the forty-year-old women
with their melancholy eyes.
This depresses me.
Woman is more alert than Man,
she thinks with her body.
With age, a man remains a beast.

At dawn, while I'm sleeping,
I sense your body slipping out of bed
and you entering the toilet
to pee, leaving
the door open.
I listen, still dozing, to the whistling
—the whistling of your pussy.

All alone at home
for the past two weeks.
I have received few telephone calls.
I empty out a can of mushrooms into the frying pan
and heat them up
without butter, without salt, without a sauce.
I eat them, standing in front of the television set,
while watching Blacks looting stores in Los Angeles.
The United States is rotting away slowly but surely.
How the devil to get rid of my melancholy!

It's been ten years since you died,
Aris Alexandrou, I haven't forgotten you,
and so I got up and went to Thiais,
the cemetery far outside of Paris,
to stand before your venerable grave,
Aris, my unforgettable friend,
and I didn't see any little bouquet
on the slab covering your coffin,
for no one,
no one, remembers this gloomy anniversary.
And today those shithead students
don't even know your name,
let alone your books.
My dear Aris, who hated you the most?
The communists? The bourgeois?

You seem bothered by all these names
that I cite in my poems.
But those women whom I loved, those friends,
are not ghosts.
And they know that I think of them all the time.

I happen to hear many Greeks
speak about their old loves:
—then I turned her ass into a smokestack!
Those ungrateful fellows forget how much
they adored that ass back then,
which gave them such joy and pleasure.
Ingratitude wounds me more
than vulgar phrases.

Beautiful women grow older.
I think that this incredible injustice
is the greatest proof
of the non-existence of God.

I smoke.
I sometimes smoke up to forty cigarettes a day.
However, often the cigarette burns out,
abandoned in the ashtray
while I muse about the women whom I have loved.

I remember very well
those excellent women
with extravagant hats,
who were painted by my contemporary
Andreas Phokas,
and whom I had seen in his house,
thirty years ago,
up there in the shadow of the Erechtheion.
However, only now have I seen the portrait
of one of those gorgeous women
ruined by wrinkles
and the ravages of old age
—I admit, tears have come to my eyes.

And you ask me:
—why don't you write beautiful poems anymore,
like those from twenty years ago?
And I think:
—but back then I was forty years old.
The closer you come to the coffin
the more you leave behind flowery phrases,
the beautiful empty words.

I have never been unhappy.
I get along well with my
innate melancholy.

I suffer from hysteria about cleanliness.
This is why I lick your asshole.

You wanted to go to Rome
because I wanted to go there,
because you knew of my passion for the Italians
and their magical language,
because I speak to you all the time about Italy.
At the end,
you understood that I am no archeologist.
As much as I adore the Villa Julia,
I love that clam casserole dish
that we ate near the Piazza di Spagna.
And I want to return to Rome.

Stupid people ask me:
—why don't you go back to Greece?
Of course, I necessarily happen to be Greek,
but my country distresses me.
I don't ever want to put my feet down in Greece again.
So I said to my wife:
—when I die like a dog, here in Paris,
burn my corpse in the crematorium
and then toss the ashes into a sewer.
This is my testament.

I tell my old far-flung stories
to Phoebe and Aristeidis.
The memories of old timers are boring.
I tell them again and again to myself,
since I struggle to understand what has happened to me
in this whore of a life I have lived.
Life is closed up like an oyster.

To give myself some pleasure today,
and only for myself,
I read one of my poems aloud.
I want to vomit.
I hate it when texts are recited
and those shitty readings
especially when idiotic actors do the recitation.
As for my poems,
one has to be sarcastic enough
to make them ridiculous.

In the old days they asked seriously:
—Live with Her in a Cabin
or live without Her in a Palace?
Today we were in the tiny room
with only a bed for two,
and fucked tenderly.
Let me gift you with the Palace.

The blonde girl lying next to me
(her naked body is fragrant)
is the plural of myself.
The past lingers in the next room.

Braque recommends:
—you need to flee from virtuosity.
Similarly, every poet
mustn't get a hard-on with words.
I'm not European because I am Mediterranean.
Therefore
I grasp the first word that comes along.

By chance she walks by in the street.
I turn around to look at her buttocks.
She seems to be dressed enough.
But the gaze of men
penetrates the thickest clothes.

I always speak from memory
without ever producing proof.
Moreover, I sense that my readers
are angered by my dirty words.
This is why
I will henceforth use only diminutives:
little pussy, little asshole, little prick, etc.
Miniatures have always been
accepted and appreciated.

I'm sleeping alone tonight.
I lean my head on the pillow
and perk my ears to my heart.
I feel nervous.
And I think:
—chase that passion from your mind
and let it slip down to your balls.
However, that damned passion
falls to my heels.

Control passion
—otherwise the poet burns.
Passion is dangerous
—it catches fire like gas.
Economize passion
—you'll need it to reach the grave.
Don't confuse passion
with ejaculation.
I want to fuck my typewriter,
since my manuscript has caught a cold.

She is sitting to my left.
She asks me what my name is.
Pumpkinopoulos, I tell her.
She asks me what my profession is.
I am retired, I reply.
A few days later, she discovered the big lie.
But she was already naked.
I told her that I admired her magnificent asshole:
—it looks like a bud.
At this, she leapt out of bed
and spread her buttocks so I could see them
in front of the mirror.
She smiles sweetly.
Her naiveté reinvigorates the erotic Mystery.

Inside Eve's pussy
Adam remains
an important man.
Outside of Eve's pussy
Adam drops back to nothing.

Epsilon who was tall like an ancient goddess,
and Theta who always got mad, and Zeta,
and Kappa with her scouring pad of a pussy,
and Delta who couldn't wait,
and Iota (alias the All-Holy),
and Alpha and that Eta,
and Sigma, and recently Beta,
and all the other ones, blondes, brunettes,
all the other remarkable ones, the unforgettable ones,
each etched with a scalpel in memory.
O endless litany of ample-assed women,
O Lofty Generous Creatures,
I owe everything to You.

Of course, of course, patience is needed
to discover the Secret City
(I mean of Brussels)
with its calm monotonous quarters.
However, I prefer the Eternal City,
the same one that Stendhal describes
in his brilliant book about Rome.
That Rome, indeed that Rome
in which you can stroll above the millennia
and whose beauty dazzles you.

> Vile, vile, abject
> is the soul of the masses,
> with its heart turned over to interest,
> with its cheek that cannot feel
>   the slaps!

That pentastich is beautiful, Mary,
but it wasn't written by me.
I asked Karyotakis for his permission
to offer you this little bouquet.
You can see how the Great Suicide,
in such solitude and despair,
stabs you brutally with his knife.

In the Latin Quarter,
across from the hideous Pantheon,
a well-known library is breathing calmly,
the Bibliothèque Sainte-Geneviève,
in its calm and dignified horizontality.
I think that it is
the most beautiful edifice in Paris.

Aretino wrote that
only the Venetians
could invent salad.
Martial already praised the Venetians
for being great gourmets.
Indeed, salad was a great invention.
The cushion, however, was even a greater one.
You can use it as a pillow
or to put your feet on it.
But, especially, to slip it beneath the stomach
of your naked Lover
lying on the bed
to make her little ass stick out.

Anything that is against the Church
rejoices me.
Anything that damages the Established Order
appeases me.
Anything that opposes Morality
is good for my health.
And because Shit is smeared over everything
I say I'm going to write, starting right now,
diabolical poems!

One after another my friends die
and I see our ranks thin out.
Elias keeps me up to date, regularly,
about the funerals of poets and painters.
I don't believe in oracles.
But now you too are throwing out evil curses:
—maybe you'll be dead next year!
My generation moves off, fades away, vanishes.
I write this brief epilogue
while our ranks thin out
—we the old geezers!

....**After**..

I've grown old.
It's better that I've grown old.
—if in this way I find some calm.

Paris, 17 January 1993

I'm disgusted by people who wear pajamas.
Pajamas make me think of petit-bourgeois interiors.
They make me think of senility and hospitals.

Paris, 17 January 1993

I thought that the ocean looked like
the Atlantic Ocean looked like the
but no, it doesn't look like the Mediterranean.
For the ocean isn't
the Atlantic Ocean isn't
absolutely isn't blue.
Because the ocean the gray
filthy blackish muddy
Atlantic Ocean
isn't the Aegean Sea that I loved.

Paris, 17 January 1993

This morning she swore
(I certify it)
she swore with tearful eyes
(we're speaking about real tears)
she swore she would stay
(and the future will show it)
she swore while staring at me
(and I was staring at her eyes)
she swore that I was the love of her life
(but this whorish life is fickle)
she swore that if she leaves it's only to come back
(ultimately, I'm the one who'll leave).

Paris, 17 January 1993

At the Atrium Café my wife and I
are drinking coffee and speaking Greek.
The unknown lady next to us wants to know
what language we were speaking and we explain.
It's at the Atrium where I would meet Aris,
Aris Alexandrou.
Today my soul saddens
every time I pass by that café.

Paris, 17 January 1993

Also gone is Pentzikis,
my cherished Mentor,
who never managed to convert me.
Pentzikis has also died—
a great Greek mind
who was disgusted by his imitators.
When my mentor died
those rats of Athens
who hated him treacherously
listened to the news in silence.
Go to hell, worthless bastards!

Paris, 17 January 1993

I adore your cunt,
but you mustn't overdo it,
because your cunt up front
is nonetheless kept withdrawn.
I see your cunt
while you cannot see it.

Paris, 17 January 1993

Those two are admiring you,
the two men sitting across from you,
and as they gaze, they're clearly charmed.
You are really beautiful.
I'm drinking my coffee at a remote table.
Hidden in the shade,
I too am dazzled,
but you're looking at the other two.

Paris, 1 February 1993

Angry, he looks at me and declares:
—all women are sluts.
My friend is perhaps a good doctor
but he senses nothing,
neither about Love, nor about Women.

Paris, 2 February 1993

I know all your little ways.
How your eyes look when you're lying.
How you cut meat with a knife.
The natural smell of your skin.
I place my head on your stomach
and your innards gurgle.
You love everything about a Woman
or nothing at all.

Paris, 2 February 1993

They say it's impossible
to stick your tongue
into the asshole of your Beloved.
But I can do it.
Without being a dog.

Paris, 3 February 1993

I rubbed my fist against your pussy,
did so for a long time.
And when our glorious fuck was over
I didn't wash my hand
so that I could sniff it late into the evening.
And every time
that the smell of your pussy hit my nostrils
my prick rose.

Paris, 3 February 1993

Poetry is a sham
and Poets are big liars.
All that exists is this Body you adore.

Paris, 3 February 1993

You keep bragging, cocksucker,
and play the big shot for me,
and you say and say again:
—see that girl? I screwed her...
I listen with reticence to your tales,
since I've always been a slave,
—I mean, the slave of Women.
And I don't consider it humiliating
to be dominated by a Woman.
A true man knows how to let things be.
Moreover, let me inform you that I'm no masochist.

Paris, 4 February 1993

You always come
along with your pussy.

Paris, 5 February 1993

Saturday, February 6th.
It's cold.
But even colder is the silent telephone.
At sixty-five, everything is melancholy.
At sixty-five, everything is shit.

Paris, 6 February 1993

I smoke like a fireman.
In this way I am free
to conquer my own cancer.

Paris, 6 February 1993

Poets should be killed
like rabid dogs.
The most cunning Poet
is a naïve person.
And for that reason, dangerous.
An Innocent person is Revolutionary.

Paris, 6-7 February 1993

—You who are so brutal, so harsh,
why do you write like this, making jokes and farces?
This is what Periklis asked me once.
And now I can answer:
—because in Literature it is easy to make readers weep
and because it's more difficult to make them smile
and because I like to make readers laugh.
Moreover, I also want to laugh.

Paris, 10 February 1993

I'm stooped over for good.
I'm misshapen from writing
and all that nonsense
and melancholy.
—an unbearable melancholy
that has haunted me ever since '44.

Coye, 12 February 1993

I don't possess the key to your pussy.
I can't explain my soul.
And everything that I breathe through my nostrils
is mixed-up
feelings of tenderness, bitterness, and rage.
Only your pussy can make me forget.

Coye, 13 February 1993

The old man has long lived in Coye.
I have run into him ever since 1976.
Today, Saturday, he's wandering around
the village fruit market.
I greet him (bonjour, Monsieur!)
and marvel: he's still alive?
And I suppose the old man
has the same secret thoughts about me.

Coye, 13 February 1993

It's midnight and I start fucking
but I can't.
Is the blockage in the balls or in the mind?
Is it this horny girl's fault?

Coye, 13 February 1993

But isn't it odd
that a cynic like me
is tormented by feelings?
Isn't this unjust?

Coye, 13 February 1993

You want me to be sincere in my writing.
My most beautiful love letters
Are these little poems that I jot down.
I see the Truth in others;
I am cross-eyed in front of my own Truth.

Coye, 13 February 1993

Ah, those mediocre fellows who think they are revolutionaries!
Ah, those fellows who wear three-piece suits!
Ah, those fellows who buy their fucks!

Coye, 13 February 1993

I have no more tears.
The rain is falling at an angle.
Stop crying over me.
It's too early.

Coye, 13 February 1993

The Coca-Cola sign is famous far and wide.
It's likely that it's even
better known than the hammer and sickle.
Old symbols eat away at our guts.
The slut of sadness is a great thief.

Coye, 13 February 1993

I'll speak about pleasant things:
about winter frost
and about young calves grazing,
about the dazzling full moon in January,
and about the babbling of a brook.
And yet
all that has come too late, at the wrong time,
with no rhyme or reason,
I rightly fear.

Coye, 13 February 1993

Sleeping deeply, I'm dreaming
and see myself in a coffin.
I have been killed, they say, by a car
and therefore someone is penally responsible.
I awake in a fright
and open the Key to Dreams
which interprets this nightmare
as a future erotic success.

14 February 1993, in the train going back to Paris

In our garden,
in the spring sunlight,
I observe ladybugs
delighted to devour
the aphids of the rose.

14 February 1993, in the taxi taking us home

You must have beautiful eyes.
Why do you wear black sunglasses?
Why hide the mystery
that clearly comes from you?

Paris, 14 February 1993

We turn at the big square
and go down the little street
to the Italian restaurant
(I don't mean a pizzeria)
and we sit down at a sidewalk table,
as usual, as usual.
Back then, this was the little café
of the old anarchists of Paris.

Paris, 14 February 1993

These mini-poems
look like breadcrumbs
or perhaps
like gold dust
—that's all.

Paris, 14 February 1993

The Poet resists
by ridiculing his own poems.
The Poet is, in fact,
nothing but the King's Fool.
The Poet is forced by society
to breathe through his asshole.
At times he is graced by a smile.

Paris, 15 February 1993

Yfantis, my Yfantis,
those mindless bastards pretend not to notice you,
but You, you know well that I know,
that I see, indeed, that you are an important Poet.
The more the Conspiration of Silence grows,
the more you can be sure
that you are honored by this Silence of the Mediocre.
And I thank You,
because I learn how to write poems
by reading all you Young Poets.

Paris, 15 February 1993

Today eroticism
seems commonplace.
As banal as the Parthenon.

Paris, 18 February 1993

Oh you, shadowy Pussy,
closed Pussy, silent Pussy,
Pussy that no longer smiles at me,
dry Pussy and angry Pussy,
I'm patient and I persist,
while waiting for you to crack open one more time
and become the Pussy that I know
—the Pussy of Reconciliation
with myself.

Paris, 18 February 1993

The day before yesterday I saw my face on television. When I saw it, I was taken with fright and I thought: who is that old geezer?

Paris, 18 February 1993

One day (going back thirty years)
Yorgos and I were listening,
I mean the late Yorgos Ioannou,
to that rebetic song that begins with the words
"Don't despair, it won't be long"
and he (bless him) turned to me and said:
—Elias, I'd be proud
if I had published such a poem.
—Yes, Yorgos, so would I,
I'd be very proud if I managed to write
with such emotion.
      For, as Gorpas says,
         the rebetic song is a masterful art.

Paris, 18 February 1993

I know.
You see me as a thistle.
Open me more deeply, and you'll find me.

Paris, 19 February 1993

You slutty Memory,
give me some peace.
Pick up your rubbish
and get out of my way,
you buttfucked Memory.

Paris, 19 February 1993

In my fatherland
a Poet gets applause
only when he commits suicide.

Paris, 19 February 1993

In fact, the Poet is a monster of nature
and the mediocre rightly reject him
and murder him.
The Poet is enigmatically present
as the world subsists in its banality.
That the Poet is even born is an accident.
Preferable are merchants and judges.

Paris, 20 February 1993

She's upset and loses her temper:
—I've been going out with him for three years;
he tortures me;
he has a little dick,
and all he does is rub it against the lips of my pussy,
it's not much fun. . .
I wonder:
—how can one balance out
a prick and emotions?

Paris, 20 February 1993

And now I going to become difficult.
And now I'm going to stop kneeling.
And now I'm going to become cheap.
And now, love of mine,
I'm going back into my hole.

Paris, 20 February 1993

..................Ten Poems for Dimitris Souliotis..................

In the Fog

Dimitris Souliotis shoots me through with riddles,
ambivalent phrases, oracles—he kills me.
Melancholy emerges as a persistent endoscopy.
Controlling my Passion means I have no Passion.
Melancholy plunges you into deep seas,
breaks you up into deep wells and unfathomable feelings.
No definition of definition has ever been invented,
but I see a melancholy person as a Pious Human Being
whose shape represents his very soul.
As an experience, perhaps Eros is a private affair
that usually takes place between Two People.
Facing Melancholy, you remain alone, all alone.
The melancholy person is an archer who constantly,
                              incessantly, hits the Black Target.
In Art, in Poetry, Thought acts as a poison.
Souliotis says: Give me a moan
and I'll make you a painting.
Paintings betray, but they must be made.
The sensitive Man fears his thorny self.
My sad heart, my heart with its black flag,
my mourning heart, my heart full of grief.
It's preferable that the spectator weeps,
yet, despite this, it's the Painter who commits suicide.
In my Fatherland, wherever you dig,
you'll find the bones of the slain.

The Boat and the Ship

You fill my soul with Your love.
The sky rises as we make love in the boat.
In the Drunken Boat and the Ship of Fools
I exist, we exist, because I love You and You love me.
In Painting, in Sculpture, what is depicted,
what is expressed, is directly sensed
but often shadowy and incomprehensible.
A Painting makes me vibrate; I refuse to interpret it.
A boat is a dreamy way of fleeing.
Alexandros Papadiamantis depicted such an escape,
when a young man and a newlywed
tried to run away from the aged groom.
From my Fatherland I want to remember, to evoke,
only beautiful things: the whitest steamers
gliding away to pearl-like islands.
If perspective were lacking, Human Beings would be blind.
I mean that the Boat with the naked Women sails like that,
racing across a sea which, I hope, is the Aegean.
The sun is shining in the golden sky,
while lanterns cast light on nightly love scenes.
The naked Woman, the Seductress who enchants Men,
the Nereid of Yialos, the Gorgon, the Sphinx, the Harpy.
I will graze on Your breasts.
The Crescent Moon is hovering over the sea
and, at times, the whore of the Full Moon
                —she sees everything, knows everything.
Eros is a crocodile that can swallow you.
One day the late Nikos Kavvadias told me:
                        and the Sea has a pussy.
I caressed Your fluffy little pink pussy
and, now, the Thousand Devils are stalking me.

The Enchanted Bed

A bed is a piece of furniture used for Giving Birth and—
and for Loving and Dying—but also for Dreaming.
The erotic bed, at times magical, at times enchanted,
somersaults and embraces the Body of the Beloved.
I sense goosebumps as Psychic vibrations,
sweet bodily goosebumps.
A Good Man worships the Body of his Beloved,
because the Woman, by offering her body,
gifts the Lover with her very soul.
The Body is burning in bed, radiating,
sending out erotic messages with winks and shudders.
Outside, an icy wind is blowing and it's snowing.
The window remains wide open
while sparse snowflakes fall into the room.
The Man, besieged for life,
sensing how the Woman calls to him through the silence,
takes his erect cock in his fist and
                            (completely hypnotized)
prepares to throw it into the Hydria of Pleasure.
Fortunate are Painters who are insolent with impunity.
Simple things have simple names
                    the bread of God
                    herbs and buds
                    cool raindrops
                    tender little pussies.
Copulation, Pleasure, overwhelmed us, exhausted us,
split the night apart and the house split apart.
Throw away the obsolete, kill the moralists.
I left at dawn, leaving my Beloved in bed.
The trees in the yard looked at me in amazement.

The Tree and the Forest

A Tree puts itself forth as the One, the Monad,
whereas a Forest is always represented as a Whole.
A Naked Woman is the opposite, without being reduced to an object.
Behind the trunk of the disheveled Tree
I can see the hidden Woman's bare feet,
and her hand is making naughty gestures.
The Dark Forest and its horrors—
                in 1951, while walking in the Chasia mountains
                under the dense foliage of the forest,
                I noticed a skeleton slouched over
                next to his machine gun.
                Of course, he was a guerrilla.
                His scalp still showed tufts of hair.
                Stunned, I walked away weeping.
Today, commemorative speeches sound like insults.
Well, you have been right for twenty years in a row,
but these twenty years have gone by without justifying yourself,
and now I see how the Nightmare nestled in your heart.
I'm crawling through the underbrush, among the ferns,
competing with amaranths and thistles,
observing like a child the ants and the lizards,
listening to the tireless cicadas,
smelling the oregano and the intoxicating mint,
and thinking of how Greece back then, how once
it looked like Crystal Lake.
In the Forest I'm not afraid of facts, but of phenomena.
A fact causes joy, sadness, thoughts, reactions.
The abyss of phenomena bayonets me.
In the small clearing of the Forest stand the Two Lovers.
They are in ecstasy, captives of their Emotions.
And the Two Lovers come back
                (yes, there, to the little tufted tree)
to hug and kiss tenderly.
Ah, what would be left to us if we lacked romance?

Naked Love

Souliotis's paintings are lightning flashes of Love.
The French say: and the most beautiful girl
can give you only what she has.
A naked Woman's weapons are irresistible.
Souliotis's erotic formulas trip, tremble,
waver between ambiguity and timidity.
Thanks to the pictural fog, the Crowd can't see you
and therefore cannot perceive the Sacred Ceremony of Pleasure.
The rose you gave me has begun to wither.
The memories of Your naked Body wound me
and I remain limp, trying to plunder my Soul.
The image of Your body fits into no piece of writing.
Lovers mingle, fuck like Gods,
because Emotions are inherent in the Senses.
Dreams are like little windows—
                    through them you enter secretly
                    and secretly read the poems
                    and leave me three flowers
                    and three thousand kisses.
The Body of the Beloved is a harp,
which requires nimble fingers, gentle gestures.
Nothing charms a Woman more
than to be loved by a Man
with a dark soul and a poetic disposition.
                    —this is what Kierkegaard wrote.
Bodies lying in bed, thighs and tresses,
feelings braided like a plait, measured words,
the kneeling Woman raises her Ass
                    (oh celestial spectacle!)
eagerly waiting for the triumphant Phallus
—her horny pussy foams and drips.
Love does not suffer from the gray matter of Thought.

A Body Falls and Falls

There is no correlation between Love and Willpower.
The Wise decisions of the Will do not dissuade Eros.
The Vulva is no Somatic sophism,
but the truly ornate Womanly Padlock is one.
This is why the erotic inspirations of the erotic Painter
start from the spine, along with Sperm.
Pour strychnine and arsenic-laced water on those wimps
and scumbags who hate Women.
Hate is neither a convenient nor a practical feeling,
and, in fact, it induces a heavy stomach and indigestion.
Come nearer, secrets, come, because I have a secret,
that I will Whisper secretly to you—
                                  let them go and get lost
                                  and may all of them vanish forever
                                  since even hedonistic fucks
                                  are also forgotten
                                  and only Your image remains.
As the Painter expresses himself symbolically,
his Chromatic range narrows.
The red Siren is swaying,
perhaps tied to the mast of the ship,
and a Couple also hovers on High in the gaping space,
until the fallen Angel collapses and falls,
                                  falls head over heels,
a seeming carcass, rather than some Youth.
I cannot decrypt the personal code
of the painting with the Knight and the Devil,
but the overturned half-naked Body is obvious
and more obvious the horse with the female rump,
which becomes completely female because the tail is missing.

The Epitaphic Body

When I first saw printed in a small format
the woodcut with a naked Woman
sitting on a horizontal plane,
I was struck severely and said:

                        Oh my, I adore You.

Later, I saw the practically gigantic woodcut
and felt the same intense emotion.
This is perhaps Souliotis's most balanced work,
in which the Painter, with a calm, rested soul,
has captured the Body of the Beloved.
The Body is depicted, directly, from behind
                    (her half-bowed head and hair,
                    her back, her arms up to the elbows,
                    her round, comfortably settled ass),
without an Idol's vain embellishments.
I hear this naked Woman whispering in my ear:
the Painter Sees Me and is Musing, He Loves Me.
Souliotis's quick simple sketch
hides an impenetrable, erotic, mournful message.
The almost square woodcut has two axes,
namely the Body and the horizontal background,
both united in an inverted Greek letter Tau.
The Body is slightly off-center and,
at the same time, the horizontal plane not completely horizontal
and this is how the work avoids any risk of seeming icy.
The center of gravity of the painting falls slightly lower,
along with the thematic focus,
softening for us the all-black background.
Already Nightmares are coming,
beating their drums and tambourines.

Here Comes the Goat-Hoofed One

Well, is the naked Woman weeping and tied to the Tomb?
Some questions receive no answers.
The background looks like a Holy Table
covered with the sacred antimins,
but also perhaps a common table with a tablecloth,
a small chest, or (why not?) a coffin, or some kind of memorial object.
The Tomb interpretation is enhanced by the dominant black color,
by the Woman's sorrow, by the diffuse Melancholy.
And yet, the woodcut emits a mute eroticism.
Souliotis, not tolerating any uniformity,
gives us a different parallel to the Theme,
which he expresses even more enigmatically.
A similar background with a bedsheet
on which sits a rather old Naked Woman,
and the Naked Woman has been ridden by the Evil Spirit,
the Goat-Hooved One of the Forest with a female ass and a tail.
And we don't know what is being asked and demanded
of the Naked Woman
by the wretched Satyr and Seilinos and Pan and the Devil.
And the Painter doesn't allow us to guess.
Doubt is crawling around like an ominous reptile.
I also reluctantly approach the Dance of Love
in which another naked Woman covers her pubis
with two wings (torn from her back),
imitating shy Cherubs.
I perk up my ears to the obscure echoes and wonder.
I sense that what is coming will be more even more obscure.

Nightmares Whip Me

A Nightmare can appear as a vague threat:
two silhouettes peeking between Trees
(they don't see the Couple who has met in the Forest)
and watching a blurry scene inscribed in a semicircle.
A Nightmare can begin as a phobia
because of imaginary animals which are present.
A Nightmare can come
from a headless corpse (or statue) with severed hands,
which someone is trying to load into a saddlebag.
I think any tapping sound is a shot
and run away in fright.
Now the fire and the knife and the bell are removed.
Dig your grave, my friend, to get to know yourself better.
Instead of so-called Freedom,
it's better to talk about Power,
while killers approach with lowered barrels.
The completely naked Old Woman is stuck in the cauldron
and no Man arouses her plucked Pussy.
Even in the coffin I'll be kicking.
You come closer and I see this as Green,
you smile at me and I reckon it to be Red,
you kiss me and the sun shines brightly.
The important Painter loses the Morals given to us,
kills the terrible force we call Habit
and with Passion strengthens his Humanness.
And when rotten Frustration arrives, he is ready for it.
Purple is considered to be a good shroud.

Behold Death

Dirt will clog my mouth
and my eye-roots will suck it.
Two Skeletons are sawing away at the Tree of Life.
The Devil is devilish and death is definitive.
Facing death, the Artist can do nothing and,
in addition, he is not entitled to extraterritoriality or even a reprieve.
The moment of death is the longest second
as well as the shortest period of our lives.
Death strikes only one blow,
leaving the useless corpse on the spot.
Patience and foxy tricks don't prevent Death,
which you must await with peace and dignity.
I think of how the curse of one who is wronged can grasp out,
but a Dead Man has no voice, no gurgling language,
to curse the impious pitiless Kharos.
Because no one can be present with him in the Tomb
—no memories, no remembrances, no amulets—
the Painter captures and keeps beyond Silence
the smiles and the bitterness, the longings and the pleasures.
The Beauty of Beauties walks on the wet grass
and the Idiot searches for her in the Forest,
holding a lighted candle in his hand
because the Full Moon half hides behind the Trees.
The brilliant Painter never laughs.
Suddenly the bathroom door opened
and Anna the Whore came out naked, like a naked sword.
Hey old geezer of a spectator,
you, who pretend to be unknowing and moral.

[Untitled]

The Devil doesn't get mixed up at all
in Kharos's whims and dirty tricks.
Souliotis depicts Kharos traditionally,
identifying him with the Death-Skeleton.
We come across the Death-Skeleton all over the world:
in early woodcuts where he appears as Sagittarius,
in the carved Macabre Dance in Rouen,
on playing cards, on various emblems,
in painted Triumphs of Death,
in cemetery skulls,
as well as in the fiestas depicted by the great Posada.
Death has stabilized its form as the Sickle-Carrier,
since he reaps the Souls of People with his scythe.
However, he goes forward to Kings kindly,
holding out an Hourglass as a convincing argument.
Kharos is a rascal, barefoot and naked.
The Death-Skeleton painted by Souliotis
is unpredictable—sometimes laughing and sneering,
sometimes coming out of a horse's ass
                    (which, of course, lacks a tail).
Death respects neither the Nereid of the Woods,
nor Cinderella nor Prince Charming.
Even the Knight stands in awe before Kharos,
who bends his arm to remind him of his scythe.
Kharos comes from Nowhere
and sends the Apostles packing to Nowhere.
Death, with its inaccessible allegories,
and supreme Love, and lurking Nightmares,
form the basis of Souliotis's issues and aesthetics.
We do not know the Skeleton's gender,
because it has neither genitals nor hair.
        Oh, my father, how young you were when you were slaughtered.

NOTES

These notes draw on Petropoulos's notes in his Poems (Ποιήματα, Nefeli, 1993) and *Never and Nothing* (Ποτέ και τίποτα, Nefeli, 1993). I have given many of, but not systematically all, the bibliographical references to each sequence or book: this information can be found in the bibliography of *Harsh out of Tenderness: The Greek Poet and Urban Folklorist Elias Petropoulos* (Cycladic Press, 2020). For English-language readers, I have also elucidated many of the references in the poems.

Funeral Oration

Petropoulos wrote this sequence (Λόγος Επικήδειος) in May, a few days after 21 April 1967, the day when a group of colonels carried off a coup d'état in Greece, initiating the "Junta" or "Dictatorship of the Colonels" (which lasted until 24 July 1974). Petropoulos evokes "hopeless hours" after he had lost his journalistic job at the newspaper *Mesimvrini* (Μεσημβρινή), as well as his home and a woman whom he loved. The sequence was first published as a "lyrical epilogue" following his essays on Greek rebetic songs in the first edition of his anthology Ρεμπέτικα Τραγούδια (1968).

When Petropoulos evokes the "rebetis" (singular) or "rebetes" (plural), he refers to an underground figure who is also sometimes called a "mangas" (singular) / "manges" (plural). In his introduction to John Taylor's translation of rebetic songs, *Rebetika: Songs from the Old Greek Underworld* (Alcyon Art Editions, 1992), he gives this colorful description: "During . . . the latter part of the nineteenth century, the *manges/rebetes* of the underworld were developing their own way of life. They frequented specific neighborhoods: in Athens, for example, one of their areas was Psiri, near the markets; among their districts in Piraeus were Karaiskaki and

Trouba; and in Thessaloniki, Vardari was a favorite hangout. In these neighborhoods they had their own tavernas and cafés, they controlled smuggling, the hashish market, the gambling clubs and the whorehouses, and trafficked in stolen goods. The *rebetes* always had their own style of dress. In the later evolution of the style, the *rebetis* wore tight trousers made of the best imported material, a dark collarless shirt usually black or purple, narrow pointed shoes with high heels, and a fedora hat pushed far back on his head, or so far forward that he had to tilt his head to see. The hat had a black band to show mourning for his victims. He carried a knife or revolver in his belt and in his hand a cane made of hard cherrywood which he could use as a weapon in fights. He wore his jacket with only the left arm in the sleeve so that he could flip it round the forearm as a shield against his opponent's knife or cane. He walked with a subtly arrogant swagger, left shoulder hunched slightly forward to keep his jacket on, often fingering a *komboloi*, and swinging only his right hand. [. . .] The *manges* trusted only *manges* and avoided dealings with other persons. The police persecuted them as an objectionable social element, and the upper and idle classes ignored them and wished they didn't exist. Their moral isolation was so complete that no Greek writer wrote about them except in terms of curses and condemnation. The Greek political Left also denounced them, even more strongly than the police, and although some articles have emerged from the Left in the past ten years [Petropoulos is writing in 1992], these articles have arbitrarily approved or condemned the songs on the basis of their political applicability. The rebetic songs are the most accessible source of information about the life and attitudes of the *rebetes*. [. . .] An important characteristic of these songs is that dance is an integral element along with the music and lyrics. [. . .] Equally important is the language. The *rebetes* spoke and still speak their own argot, which is exceptionally rich in expressions and hand gestures. The songs draw both from this argot as well as from the language of the working class Greeks, and it is this mixed language that constitutes the poetic expression of *rebetika*."

General Yiannis Makriyannis (1797-1864) was a Greek Independence War hero and the author of a volume of *Memoirs* (first published in 1907) in self-taught demotic Greek which is now considered a classic of Modern Greek literature.

Vassilis Tsitsanis (1915-1984) was one of the greatest rebetic song composers and bouzouki players.

Mikis Theodorakis (1925-2021) was a major Greek composer, some of whose compositions draw on rebetic songs. He was also active in Greek politics.

In the aforementioned English selection of rebetic songs, Petropoulos adds this definition of the *zeybekiko* dance (sometimes spelled *zembekiko*): "The *zeybekiko* is the manges' favorite dance. It is danced alone in a tense, melancholic manner. As an evening in the taverna progresses, the *zeybekiko* dancer will sometimes perform certain stunts, such as picking up café tables with his teeth, drinking from a glass on the floor without using his hands, pulling out a knife thrust in the floor with his teeth, or dancing with a wine bottle or hookah on his head."

Yannis Tsarouchis (1910-1989) was a Greek painter known for his erotic and homoerotic paintings. One of Petropoulos's first books, *Ελύτης Μόραλης Τσαρούχης* (*Elytis Moralis Tsarouchis*, privately printed, 1966 / Pleias, 1975 / Grammata, 1980 / Patakis, 1996), was devoted to Tsarouchis, Yiannis Moralis (1916-2009), and the collages made by the poet Odysseus Elytis (1911-1996).

Body

This long poem (*Σώμα*) was written in the spring of 1969 and first published in a bilingual album by the artist Pavlos Moskhidis, with an English translation by Nikos Germanacos. The poem subsequently appeared in the magazine *Tram* (Nos. 3-4, February 1972). Petropoulos was imprisoned for five months in 1972 because of one line in *Body*: "I forget even my fatherland in front of a young naked female body." This is a new translation of *Body*.

"Give not that which is holy unto the dogs, neither cast ye your pearls before swine, lest they trample them under their feet, and turn again and rend you." Matthew 7:6 (King James Version).

In Greek mythology, Amalthea, a goat, was Zeus's nurse (and wetnurse), during the years when he was hidden from his father, Cronus, in a cave on the island of Crete. One day, Zeus accidently broke off one of Amalthea's horns while he was playing with her. To make up for the loss, he made sure that the broken horn would always be full of whatever its owner desired. The "Horn of Amalthea" is therefore the Cornucopia, the horn of abundance.

The Lernaean Hydra is the serpentine water monster in Greek mythology. The Peloponnesian site of Lerna was considered to be an entrance to the underworld.

Suicide

This long poem (*Αυτοκτονία*) was written during a "sinister night" (22-23 February 1970) in the convalescence room of Kassandras Prison. *Suicide* was secretly printed towards the end of October 1973 in the Tolidis Brothers' printing shop. The poem later appeared as a small book in Paris, in 1976, in a French translation by Jean-François Trocmé, with a lithograph by Alekos Fassianos.

Petropoulos uses the palindrome ΝΙΨΟΝΑΝΟΜΗΜΑΤΑΜΗΜΟΝΑΝΟΨΙΝ. Attributed to Saint Gregory of Nazianzus, the phrase means "wash the sins, not only the face." It is found on a holy water font in front of Hagia Sophia in Constantinople (Istanbul). Petropoulos then modifies the palindrome and makes a pun.

Five Erotic Poems

Written in Athens on 26 January 1974, the *Five Erotic Poems* (*Πέντε Ερωτικά Ποιήματα*) were first printed in the summer of 1975 with illustrations by the Greek artist Yiorgos Sikeliotis (1917-1984).

"The pagan from Skiathos" is the writer Alexandros Papadiamantis (1851-1911), whose short stories Petropoulos admired and often cited in his books.

Manto Aravantinou (1930-1998) was a Greek poet, known as well for her translations of James Joyce.

The "Other One who killed himself" is the Greek poet Kostas Karyotakis (1896-1928), who shot himself in Preveza, a coastal town on the Ambracian Gulf.

Kostas Mavroudis (b. 1948) is a Greek poet, short-story writer, and travel writer.

Nikos Karouzos (1926-1990) was a Greek poet noted for his religious, philosophical and metaphysical themes.

Manolis Xexakis (b. 1948), as a young poet, was encouraged by Petropoulos. His long sequence *Captain Super Priovolos* is available online, in John Taylor's translation, in *International Literary Quartery* (No. 18), and Taylor's essay "Manolis Xexakis' *Captain Super Priovolos*: Notes for an Exegesis" can be found in *A Little Tour through European Poetry* (Transaction Publishers, 2015).

Dionysios Solomos (1798-1857) is considered to be the national poet of Greece because of his poem "Hymn to Liberty," which is based on the Greek War of Independence against the Ottoman Empire (1821) and which is used as the national anthem of both Greece and Cyprus. See more information about Solomos below, in the note for *Inaccessible Tsoclis*.

Andreas Embirikos (1901-1975) was a Greek poet and also one of the first Greek psychoanalysts. He is noted for his surrealism, his radical writing style, and the erotic contents of his texts.

Tsoclis's Tree

Tsoclis's Tree (*Το Δέντρο του Τσόκλη*) was written in Paris on 4 April 1982. This text was published in the form of an art album by the Jackson Gallery (New York), with a translation by John Taylor.

Costas Tsoclis (b. 1930) is a Greek artist who long lived in Paris (before returning to Greece) and who often collaborated with Petropoulos on his projects.

A story about this painting across the room from Petropoulos's desk is told in *Harsh out of Tenderness*, pp. 122-123.

Tsoclis's apartment was located on the rue des Écouffes, which runs into the rue des Rosiers. This is the most famous Jewish quarter of Paris and several bakeries sell pastries such as those evoked here.

Mirror for You

Καθρέφτης γιά Σένα Written in Paris towards the end of 1982. Published at the Atelier Mérat (Paris) in a bibliophilic edition illustrated by Alekos Fassianos and translated by John Taylor.

In Berlin

In Berlin was first published at the Atelier Mérat in Paris in 1987, in John

Taylor's translation, as a bibliophilic album with illustrations by the artist Michael Bastow (b. 1943). The subtitle was *Notebook 1983-1984*, which refers to Petropoulos's one-year stay in Berlin at the Künstlerhaus Bethanian. The stay left an indelible mark on him and its traces are visible in subsequent articles and books, notably Η μυθολογία του Βερολίνου (The Mythology of Berlin, Nefeli, 1991). In *Harsh out of Tenderness*, this observation: "Reflect on those twenty-eight years of French exile during which [Petropoulos] so intently continued to get down on paper some forty-seven years of experience in Greece. His folkloristic projects about France notwithstanding (and most were not finalized), Greece remained his obsession. Perhaps tellingly, perhaps simply because opportunities arose at the right time, he published several articles and two books, *In Berlin* and *The Mythology of Berlin*, based on the research that he undertook, and on his personal experiences, during his one-year sojourn in Berlin. This body of work is comparatively more copious than what he wrote in regard to France." The reader of these notebook poems and fragments will notice, however, that Petropoulos uses a few French words and expressions even in a German context.

The Totenkopf Division was the SS unit responsible for administrating the Nazi extermination camps.

Man Ray (1890-1976), the American visual artist and photographer.

Hermann Nitsch (1938-2022) was an Austrian artist associated with the Vienna Actionist group, oriented towards performance, as well as with the Orgies-Mysteries-Theater whose plays and happenings are designed to provoke disgust in the spectator before catharsis.

Oswald Wiener (1935-2021) was an Austrian writer, theoretical linguist, and jazz musician (to mention only a few of his activities). He is associated with the Wiener Gruppe (Vienna Group) of radical experimental writers and poets.

Otto Dix (1891-1969), the German expressionist painter.

The Good Person of Szechuan (1938-1940) is a play written in exile by Bertolt Brecht (1898-1956), with the collaboration of Margarete Steffin (1908-1941). The play presents a critique of capitalism.

King Constantine II of Greece (1940-2023) was the last king of Greece. In December 1967, after failing to carry off a counter-coup d'état against the Colonels who had seized power, he went into exile. The monarchy was abolished in 1973.

The French expression "malbaisé(e)," literally "badly fucked," refers to someone who is sexually frustrated.

"*Riko-Riko-Ebiriko*" refers to Andreas Embirikos—see note to *Five Erotic Poems*. The "twelve commandments" are found in Exodus 20:2-17 and in Deuteronomy 5:6-21.

"TÜRKEN RAUS" and "JUDEN RAUS" respectively mean kick the Turks and the Jews out of Germany. Petropoulos is of course referring in this poem to the two sides of the Berlin Wall, which divided West Berlin from East Berlin and which would come down only on 9 November 1989.

Fritz Gilow (1945-2004) was a German sculptor and installation artist.

In traditional Arabic, Kurdish, Greek, Middle Eastern, or Turkish music, a "taqsim" is usually a solo prelude played before the main performance. I have adopted the spelling "taxim."

Kurt Tucholsky (1890-1935) was a German journalist and novelist who spoke out against the rise of National Socialism. His books were among the first to be burnt by the Nazis. He fled to Sweden in 1933 and two years later committed suicide.

"déshabillez-vous" means "take off your clothes!"

The "Ode to Walt Whitman" (1930) by the Spanish poet Federico Garcia Lorca (1898-1936) is known for its explicit evocation of homosexuality and, indeed, presumed homophobia.

Yiannis Ritsos (1909-1990), the Greek poet often associated with the Greek Left.

Rosa Luxemburg (1871-1919) and Karl Liebknecht (1871-1919), the two Spartacus League revolutionaries who were assassinated on 15 January 1919. Their bodies were thrown into the Landwehr Canal.

Messaoud Chebbi (b. 1954) is a Tunisian photographer and collage artist.

The novel *The Room* (1937) by the American novelist Hubert Selby, Jr. (1928-2004) expresses the sentiments of a nameless petty criminal.

Allen Ginsberg (1926-1997), the American poet and co-founder of the Beat Generation.

Estrongo Nachama (1918-2000) was a Greek singer whose musical talent kept him from being exterminated at Auschwitz, where the rest of his family was murdered. After the war, he met and married a German woman and moved to Berlin. He became internationally famous for his singing and for his efforts to promote dialogue between Jews and Christians. Nachama was born in Thessaloniki, the town in which Petropoulos grew up, beginning in 1934. Petropoulos devoted many articles and books to Thessaloniki, and several specifically to the Jewish population of the town during the 1930s and their plight during the Second World War: *Les Juifs de Salonique / In Memoriam / The Jews of Salonica* (translated into French and English by Françoise Daviet and John Taylor, Atelier Mérat, 1983) and *A Macabre Song*, postscriptum by Pierre Vidal-Naquet, translated by John Taylor, Atelier Mérat, 1985). Of particular interest is an article, which initially appeared in French, about his memories of Jewish friends and acquaintances during his childhood: "Ah, Allegra" (translated into French by Patricia Portier and Socrate C. Zervos, *Salonique 1850-1918*, Autrement, 1992, pp. 16-19).

The French expression "quel culot!" means "what nerve!"

The French expression "qui font boutique de leur cul" means "who make a showcase of their asses."

Letter to A. Kanavakis

Petropoulos notes that this sequence of four poems (*Επιστολή στον Α. Καναβάκη*) was written in Paris on 11 February 1988. First published in *Poems* (1993).

Anakreon Kanavakis (b. 1938) is a Greek painter, cartoonist, and graphic designer.

Pietro Aretino (1492-1556) was an Italian writer, playwright, poet, and satirist, noted for his outspoken homosexuality and attacks against political power. Petropoulos and Mary Koukoules translated Aretino's *Sonetti lussuriosi* into Modern Greek (*Τα Ακόλαστα Σονέτα του Αρετίνου*, Nefeli, 1992).

Giacomo Casanova (1725-1798), famous for his *Story of My Life*, was one of Petropoulos's favorite authors, as he recalls in *In Berlin*.

Félicien Rops (1833-1898) was a Belgian artist associated with Symbolism. He was championed by Charles Baudelaire, among others.

Guido Crepax (1933-2003) was an Italian cartoonist especially known for his Valentina series of books and comic strips, which combined eroticism and dreamlike narratives. His work was also often politically commited.

Tom Wesselmann (1931-2004) was an American artist noted, among other paintings, for his "Great American Nude" series.

Inaccessible Tsoclis

Written in Paris on 17-19 January 1990 and 17-21 March 1990, *Ο απρόσιτος Τσόκλης* was published bilingually in the catalogue *Tsoclis* (Athens: Adam Editions, 1992), with an English translation by Eve Jackson. This new translation has borrowed some lines from Jackson's version. The album *Tsoclis* includes illustrations of the *Medea* series of triptychs as well as scenes from the video projection, from the 1989 exhibit in Troyes.

Anton Chekhov (1860-1904), the Russian writer whose stories Petropoulos much admired. The cited words come from his letter to his brother Alexander Pavlovich Chekhov on 11 April 1889. The context is not without interest for Petropoulos's own poetics: "Try to be original in your play and as clever as possible; but don't be afraid to show yourself foolish; we must have freedom of thinking, and only he is an emancipated thinker who is not afraid to write foolish things. Don't round things out, don't polish—but be awkward and impudent. Brevity is the sister of talent. Remember, by the way, that declarations of love, the infidelity of husbands and wives; widows', orphans', and all other tears, have long since been written up. The subject ought to be new, but there need be no "fable." And the main thing is—father and mother must eat. Write. Flies purify the air, and plays—the morals." (Anton Chekhov, *Letters on the Short Story, the Drama and other Literary Topics*, selected and edited by Louis S. Friedland, Minton, Balch & Co., 1924, pp. 170-80.)

In the original Greek version of this text, when Petropoulos refers to the "Greek-Jewish poet Salomon," he writes "Salomon" in the Roman alphabet. Long after writing *Funeral Oration* (see above), Petropoulos speculated about Solomos's possible Jewish origins in his article "Ο Σαλομόν" (Salomon: On Dionysios Solomos), which was published in the newspaper *Kyriakatiki Eleftherotypia* (*Κυριακάτικη Ελευθεροτυπία*, 24 September 2000) and then republished in *Philologiki Selida* (*Φιλολογική Σελίδα*, 30 September 2000), and finally included in *Ο κουραδοκόφτης* (*The Shit-Cutter*, or *The G-String*).

When Petropoulos refers to Homer's *Nekyia* (the common name for the eleventh book of *The Odyssey* in classical antiquity), he is thinking more generally of the term "nekyia" as necromancy, that is, conversing with the dead by means of a ritual during which the dead are conjured up and questioned about the future. In the eleventh book (lines 90-94), Odysseus has journeyed to Hades, wonders how he might find his way to Ithaca, and consults with the ghost of the priest and prophet Teiresias, who asks him: "Why have you left the sunlight, to view the dead in this joyless place?"

An Encomium to Cicciolina

Τσιτσολίνας Εγκώμιον was written in Paris, 15-20 April 1991. First published in the special issue on "Vulgarité" of the *Revue de l'Université de Bruxelles* (Nos. 1-2, 1991), in a French translation by Sokratis K. Zervos. Petropoulos writes: "This [text] is no rough draft. With this chilly lyrical text I wanted to offer a flower to beautiful women, who so generously accept to let their beauty be seen and delighted in."

Cicciolina (b. 1951) is a pornographic film actress and was a deputy in the Italian parliament (1987-1991).

Phyrne (b. ca. 371 B.C.) was a courtesan. Her real name was Mnesarate ("commemorating virtue"), but because of her yellowish complexion, she was called Phyrne ("toad"). She is best known for her trial on charges of impiety. During the trial, Hypereides, the orator, fearing an unfavorable outcome, removed her robe and bared her breasts to arouse the judges' pity. Her beauty instilled a superstitious fear in them and they decided not to sentence to death "a prophetess and priestess of Aphrodite." She was acquitted.

Félicien Rop's "Pornocratès" is a painting (1878).

Jacques Sternberg (1923-2006) was a Belgian French-language writer.

Gershon Legman (1917-1999) was an American cultural critic known for his original research on limericks, dirty jokes, and erotic folklore. He lived in France, beginning in 1953, and Petropoulos knew him well. Legman wrote the introduction to Mary Koukoules's *Loose-Tongued Greeks: A Miscellany of Neo-Hellenic Erotic Folklore* (Digamma, 1983), translated by John Taylor. Petropoulos was unable to see Legman's six-volume autobiography, which started to become available only in 2016.

Ivo Andrič (1892-1975), born in Bosnia into a Croat family and later associated with Serbian literature, was a preeminent Yugoslav novelist known for his evocations of Balkan life.

The medieval police novel *The Name of the Rose* (1980) by the Italian semiotician Umberto Eco (1932-2016) was an international bestseller.

Four Seasons: Roland Topor
These four texts are dated 14-20 December 1990.

Roland Topor (1938-1997) was a French artist, writer, poet, actor, and filmmaker (to mention only a few of his trades). He illustrated the cover of Petropoulos's album *Les Juifs de Salonique / In Memoriam / The Jews of Salonica* (Atelier Mérat, 1983). In subsequent years, Topor contributed illustrations to other books by Petropoulos.

Abram Topor (1903-1992) was Roland Topor's father and also an artist.

Jacques Vallet (b. 1939) is a French poet, writer, and literary critic. His friendship with Petropoulos dates from the years in which he founded and published *Le fou parle* (1977-1984), a magazine devoted to art, literary texts, and book reviews. Petropoulos was close to Vallet and the magazine, and two chapters from *The Good Thief's Manual* (Εγχειρίδιον του καλού κλέφτη, Nefeli, 1979 / 1990) appeared, in a French translation, in the 15th issue (December 1980). Roland Topor played an important role in this magazine, in that he solicited artwork from his many artist-friends to illustrate the covers or the inside pages. Vallet is also the co-translator, with Mary Koukoules, of Petropoulos's poetry volumes Ποτέ και τίποτα / *Jamais et rien* (Nefeli, 2004) and Μετά / *Après* (Nefeli, 2004).

Olivier O. Olivier (1931-2011) was a French artist, associated (like Roland Topor) with the Panique group of artists, then with the Collège de Pataphysique and Oupeinpo (Ouvroir de peinture potentielle). He was a regular contributor to *Le fou parle*.

Yüksel Arslan (1933-2017) was a Turkish artist who began living in Paris in the 1960s, indeed in an apartment on the rue Thouin, which was located near Petropoulos's apartment on the rue Mouffetard. He became known for his "artures," which were paintings produced by using a medieval recipe based on natural materials. Among other books, he carried off the tour de force of illustrating Karl Marx's *Das Kapital*. He was a regular contributor to *Le fou parle*. Jacques Vallet devoted a three-volume work to Arslan's art, *L'Homme*.

Komet (b. 1941) is a Turkish artist who has lived in Paris since 1971.

Selçuk Demirel (b. 1954) is a Turkish artist and political cartoonist who settled in Paris in 1978. His political drawings have appeared in newspapers worldwide. Among the many books and book covers that he has illustrated is Mary Koukoules's aforementioned *Loose-Tongued Greeks: A Miscellany of Neo-Hellenic Erotic Folklore*.

Marianne has symbolized the French republic since the French Revolution.

Yujiro Otsuki (b. 1948) is a Japanese artist who lives in Paris.

"with the traditional triple kiss". In France, when one embraces another person, one gives two, three or four kisses on the cheek, depending on the region and on intimacy.

Roman Cieslewicz (1930-1996) was a Polish graphic artist and photographer who settled in France in 1963. He was also a contributor to *Le fou parle*.

"La seule revolte individuelle consiste à survivre" means "The only individual revolt consists in surviving." Topor's aphorism is found in *Petit Mémento Panique* (1965).

Viva la muerte (1970) is a film by the Spanish poet, writer, and filmmaker Fernando Arrabal (b. 1932). The film uses illustrations by Topor.

"I'd like to speak to Mlle Marguerite Duras." Petropoulos satirizes the French novelist (1914-1996) in *The Good Thief's Manual*, notably calling her "Durat" in the chapter on "pordology": "Personally, I defend the viewpoint that men fart more than women. The leader of the Women's Liberation Movement, Miss Marguerite Durat, has an opinion diametrically opposed to mine. I would like to add, however, that a beautiful woman who farts *in public* loses much of her charm. Male Chauvinists and Feminists (and, I hope, Homosexuals as well) agree on one point: *a fart is, fundamentally, a musical event.*"

Isaac Babel (1894-1940), the Russian novelist executed after being accused of denigrating Stalin.

"Vagina Dentata." Petropoulos refers to the folktale, found in several cultures, in which the vagina is said to have teeth and thus to be a threat to a man involved in sexual intercourse.

"parce que / c'est une bonne façon de m'arrêter de fumer" means "because it's a good way for me to stop smoking." In the original Greek poem, Petropoulos quotes the words in French.

Abidin Dino (1913-1993) was a Turkish artist who lived in Paris. He was especially known for his drawings of hands and flowers.

Never and Nothing

Ποτέ και τίποτα (Nefeli, 1993), with a preface by John Taylor and collages by Petropoulos. The original English version of John Taylor's preface ("Poetry, Anti-Poetry, and Disgust") is comprised in *Into the Heart of European Literature* (Transaction Publishers, 2008). The Greek collection was republished separately and posthumously as Ποτέ και τίποτα / *Jamais et rien* (Nefeli, 2004), a bilingual edition with the French translation made by Mary Koukoules and Jacques Vallet, and with photos by Phaedon Koukoules. In the Greek edition, Petropoulos notes that the poems were written on 2 May 1992.

Jordan Plevnes (b. 1953) is a North-Macedonian writer and diplomat. During the years 2000-2005 he served as the ambassador of the Republic of Macedonia to France. A selection of Petropoulos's poems, translated by Mary Koukoules and Plevnes's wife Liljana Kotevska-Plevnes, appeared in Skopje in 1993. Petropoulos was interested in the Greece-Macedonia conflict over the name of the country and was outspoken in favor of Macedonia. See "Η Μακεδονία του Ηλία Πετρόπουλου" (Elias Petropoulos's Macedonia: An Interview with Jordan Plevnes, Κυριακάτικη Ελευθεροτυπία, 8 February 2009).

For Phyrne, see above.

José Carlos Rodriguez Najar (b. 1945) is a Peruvian poet who was one of the founders of the "Hora Zero" movement in Peruvian poetry in the 1970s.

Alberto Moravia (1907-1990), the Italian novelist. Petropoulos often wore ties. In *Harsh out of Tenderness*, I cite this poem and write: "Replace 'Moravia' with 'Petropoulos.'" Even more striking than Petropoulos's elegant ties (as an object of apparel that would catch the onlooker's eye) was the overall impression that he created whenever he entered a crowded art gallery for an evening opening: his vigorous salt-and-pepper beard, his eyebrows (which tended to spring up at the ends), his striking tie of course, but also his refined three-piece suit and his perfectly ironed (perhaps even starched) shirt. I remember well his knit ties. . ." But one of the reasons behind Petropoulos's elegance, which he kept up whenever outside of his apartment, was that after six or seven years of living in France, he no longer had a *carte de séjour* (the French equivalent of a residency permit). He thought that dressing up would make him look like a university professor and would keep him from being stopped on streets by a policeman and asked for his papers. Similarly, until the Socialist Party came to power in 1981 and banned first-class cars from the Paris métro system, Petropoulos would always ride in a first-class car.

Philolaos Tioupas (1923-2010) was a Greek sculptor who long lived and worked in France.

Aris Alexandrou (1922-1979) was a Greek writer, poet, and translator of Russian literature. During the Second World War, he was briefly involved with a resistance group against the Nazi occupation of Greece, but when the group was integrated into the hierarchy of the Communist Party, he resigned. Although he did not participate directly in the Greek Civil War, he was arrested and incarcerated in prison camps. He was also imprisoned for draft dodging in 1952 and served a prison sentence of six years. When the Junta came to power in 1967, he moved to Paris where he died thirteen years later. His only novel, *Το Κιβώτιο* (*Mission Box*, 1974), which evokes the Civil War, is considered a classic.

Andreas Fokas (b. 1928) is a Greek artist noted for his realistic paintings.

". . . toss the ashes into a sewer." Petropoulos's request was put into effect after his cremation at the Père Lachaise Cemetery on 13 September 2003. For an eyewitness account, see *Harsh out of Tenderness*, pp. 164-167.

Stendhal's book about Rome is *Promenades dans Rome* (1829).

For Karyotakis, see above.

For Aretino, see above.

Martial (born between 38-41-died between 102-104) was a Roman poet famous for his satirical and erotic epigrams.

"Elias keeps me up to date, regularly, / about the funerals of poets and painters." Petropoulos refers to the short-story writer Elias Papadimitrakopoulos (b. 1930). The two men were close friends, wrote a book together (*Επιστολαί προς* μνηστήν [Letters to a Fiancée], illustrated by Alekos Fassianos, Grammata, 1980), and Papadimitrakopoulos's wife Niobe was the sister of Petropoulos's first wife. In English, see Papadimitrakopoulos's *Toothpaste with Chlorophyll / Maritime Hot Baths* (Coyote Arts, 2020), translated by John Taylor.

After

Μετά constitutes the second section of the 1993 Nefeli edition of Ποτέ και τίποτα (above). The collection was republished separately and posthumously as *Μετά / Après* (Nefeli, 2004), a bilingual edition with the French translation made by Mary Koukoules and Jacques Vallet, and with photos by Phaedon Koukoules.

Nikos Gabriel Pentzikis (1908-1993) was Petropoulos's mentor. See Petropoulos's first book: *Νίκος Γαβριήλ Πεντζίκης* (privately printed, 1958 / Grammata, 1980, with reproductions of paintings by Pentzikis / expanded edition: Athens: Patakis, 1998).

Periklis Korovesis (1941-2020) was a journalist and an author (who notably wrote about being tortured during the Junta. In 2007, he was elected to the Greek Parliament as a member of the Coalition of the Radical Left (Syriza Party), but was not reelected in 2009.

"The old man has long lived in Coye." Coye-la-Forêt, north of Paris, where Petropoulos and Mary Koukoules had a house.

"I'll speak about pleasant things." Petropoulos is offering an echo of C. P. Cavafy's poem "Morning Sea" (as translated by Edmund Keeley and Philip Sherrard, *C. P. Cavafy: Collected Poems*, Princeton University Press, 1975):

> Let me stop here. Let me, too, look at nature awhile.
> The brilliant blue of the morning sea, of the cloudless sky,
> the shore yellow: all lovely,
> all bathed in light.
>
> Let me stand here. And let me pretend I see all this.
> (I actually did see it for a minute when I first stopped.)
> and not my usual day-dreams here too,
> my memories, those sensual images.

The Italian restaurant is "La Capannina," located near the Panthéon in Paris.

Yannis Yfantis (b. 1949), like Manolis Xexakis (see above), is a younger Greek poet whom Petropoulos championed.

Yorgos Ioannou (1927-1985) was a Greek poet and writer. Petropoulos and Ioannou had a complex friendship going back to their earliest years as writers. For this poem, it is important to know that the two men feuded in 1982 because of several negative passages about Petropoulos in Ioannou's article "Δέκα Πεζά Κείμενα" (Ten Prose Texts, Φυλλάδιο, Nos. 5-6, 1982, pp. 33-37, 45, 61-62, 65, 71). Petropoulos recalls a conversation with Ioannou.

Thomas Gorpas (1935-2003) was a Greek poet and writer.

Ten Poems for Dimitris Souliotis

Petropoulos notes that the poems were written in Paris on 11-13 October 1998.

Dimitris Souliotis (b. 1966) is a Greek artist who has lived in Paris since the early 1990s. For an introduction in English to his work, see John Taylor's monograph *Dimitris Souliotis* (Titanium / Yiayiannos Gallery, 2007).

"The Drunken Boat" (1871) is the famous long poem by the French poet Arthur Rimbaud (1854-1891).

The Ship of Fools is the novel *Das Narrenschiff* (1494) by the German humanist Sebastian Brandt (1458-1521).

For the Greek short-story writer Alexandros Papadiamantis, see above.

Nikos Kavvadias (1910-1975) was a Greek writer, poet, and sailor, admired for his poetry and prose based on his sea experiences.

The French expression "la plus belle fille du monde ne peut donner que ce qu'elle a," which Petropoulos modifies by adding the "you," is attributed to Nicolas Chamfort (1741-1794), with "femme" instead of "fille." Maxim 383: "It is commonly said that 'the most beautiful woman in the world can give only what she has.' This is very false: she gives exactly what a person thinks he is receiving, because in this aspect of life, it is the imagination that fixes the value of what one receives."

"Kharos" or "Charos" is a modern Greek folklore figure deriving from the ancient Greek Charon. Many rebetic songs evoke Kharos.

José Guadalupe Posada Aguilar (1852-1913) was a Mexican painter famous for his use of skulls and skeletons in his political and cultural satire.

In Rouen, the "danse macabre" is found in the Aître Saint-Maclou, a charnel house and ossuary going back to the Black Plague of 1348. The columns in the east and west galleries are covered with couples depicted in an allegorical "dance of death."

About Elias Petropoulos

Elias Petropoulos (1928-2003) was the most controversial Greek writer of the twentieth century. Imprisoned three times during the Junta (1967-1974) and persecuted by Greek judges as late as the 1980s, this "urban folklorist" produced a vast and groundbreaking oeuvre that continues to provoke extreme reactions from readers. The author of some seventy books on topics ranging from prisons, brothels, graveyards, hats, mustaches, homosexual slang and Turkish coffee to rebetic songs, architecture and the plight of Greek Jews during the Second World War, Petropoulos was also and perhaps above all a poet. He wrote his first long poetic sequence, *Funeral Oration*, when he was thirty-nine years old, just after the Colonels had seized power. In the following decades, most of which were spent in exile in Paris (where he began living in 1975), Petropoulos produced more poetry, often in spurts of highly concentrated energy. These sequences were often initially published in rare bibliophilic editions illustrated by his artist-friends. In Greece, Nefeli Editions has gathered his poetry in *Poems* (1980 / 1993), *Four Seasons* (1991), and a double collection: *Never and Nothing* and *After* (1993). This English-language edition, *Mirror for You: Collected Poems (1967-1999)*, which includes ten poems written in 1999 about the art of Dimitris Souliotis, represents the first time that Petropoulos's poetry has been made available in English.

About John Taylor

Born in Des Moines in 1952, John Taylor has lived in France since 1977. In 2020, Cycladic Press published his memoir about working with Elias Petropoulos in Paris: *Harsh out of Tenderness: The Greek Poet and Urban Folklorist Elias Petropoulos*. Taylor has translated the short stories of Elias Papadimitrakopoulos, the poetic prose of Manolis Xexakis, and the poetry of Veroniki Dalakoura. He is also a noted translator of many key French, Swiss, and Italian poets, including Philippe Jaccottet, Jacques Dupin, Pierre-Albert Jourdan, Louis Calaferte, Georges Perros, Catherine Colomb, José-Flore Tappy, Pierre Voélin, Lorenzo Calogero, Alfredo de Palchi, and Franca Mancinelli. He is the author of several volumes of short prose and poetry, most recently *Remembrance of Water & Twenty-Five Trees* (The Bitter Oleander Press), a "double book" co-authored with the Swiss poet Pierre Chappuis, *A Notebook of Clouds & A Notebook of Ridges* (The Fortnightly Review Press), and *Transizioni* (LYRIKS Editore), issued bilingually in Italy and illustrated by Alekos Fassianos.